Kathryn —
May your life be filled
with love!
Chad Stone

The Love Magnet Rules

101 Tips for Meeting, Dating,

and Keeping a New Love

Chad Stone

SOULMATE MEDIA

The Love Magnet Rules

101 Tips for Meeting, Dating, and Keeping a New Love

Chad Stone

For more information about Chad Stone—and his books, dating and relationships advice, blog, and more—please visit www.chadstone.us

"Like" Chad Stone's Facebook page at www.facebook.com/ChadStoneAuthor

www.soulmatemedia.com

For my wife,
the love of my life.

Praise for *The Love Magnet Rules*

"What a great book of ways to attract love to you! Chad Stone has outlined a methodical, tested way to find the love of your life. His stories—including his personal ones—are inspiring and heartwarming. The Love Magnet Rules is an easy, illuminating read not to be missed."

—Kathryn Alice, author of *Love Will Find You*

"As a dating and divorce blogger and columnist, I get e-mails daily asking for advice. The biggest question I am asked is, 'How do I meet someone and fall in love?' Reading *The Love Magnet Rules* answers that question completely. With 101 tips on meeting, dating and staying in love, Chad Stone isn't offering theory, but rather practical advice that women and men can put into use. *The Love Magnet Rules* is a fantastic read for anyone who really wants to find love, but needs ideas on how to make it happen. Love it!"

—Jackie Pilossoph, DivorcedGirlSmiling.com

"Chad Stone has crafted easy-to-follow steps for meeting and keeping your long-awaited soul mate. If you're ready to find the love-of-your-life partner you've been hoping for, then now is the time to read *The Love Magnet Rules*!"

—Dr. Jane Greer, New York–based relationship expert
author of *What About Me?*
Stop Selfishness from Ruining Your Relationship

Introduction

Everyone wants to fall in love and stay in love. Being in love is magical and wonderful. It has been said that love makes the world go 'round, which is probably true. But even more important is the fact that love makes every day richer, fuller, and more enjoyable. Quite simply, love is what makes life worth living.

We all want to find that one special person who is the perfect match for us. We all want someone to share our journey through life—someone who will always be there for us. This lover is the one person who can make each day better by sharing our joys and happiness and also comforting us in times of stress and sorrow.

Unfortunately, looking for "The One" can be baffling and challenging. The process of finding the right romantic partner can seem so random. Successfully meeting our partner, and then bonding with him or her, might be the single most important thing we do during our entire life. Yet we approach it haphazardly. We take classes to learn about practically everything that's important in life—reading, writing, driving, cooking, learning work skills, and more. But we don't take any classes in how to find the love of our life—or how to keep our romantic relationship alive. Instead, we wing it. And that makes no sense whatsoever.

It's no wonder so many people are still single. We simply don't know what we're doing when it comes to meeting, dating, and keeping a new love.

Before I started working on *The Love Magnet Rules*, I was not what you would call a "deep thinker" on the subject of relationships. I *should* have understood what love is, how to find it, and how to keep it once I found it. After all, I had been married for many years. All my life I had observed and interacted with women. But I never really understood the way women think and what makes them tick. And I never really understood the fundamental differences between men and women—particularly when it comes to how they express love and commitment, and what they are looking for in a loving relationship.

After my marriage ended and my divorce was final, I had lots of time to reflect on love. Gradually, it occurred to me that I did not fully understand love, relationships, the chemistry of attraction, and the different styles that men and women use to interact with one another. I realized that if I was going to attract a new relationship to my life, I had better learn what love really is and how to attract it.

So I began to pay attention. I observed women interacting with men. I talked to female friends and acquaintances, and I asked them what they liked (and disliked) about men. I talked to men to find out what they knew (or thought they knew) about women. I read psychology books. I read books about relationships, dating, and interpersonal communication. Every time I had the opportunity, I asked women and men what they had learned about love.

Slowly, I began to formulate an understanding of what men and women want—especially the qualities they want in a romantic partner.

The deeper I got into the subject of relationships, the more I realized that men and women want a lot of the same things. Sure, we go about searching for love in different ways, and there are differences in how men and women talk about and express their commitment to their significant others. But we all want to fall in love—and live in love for the rest of our lives.

During my second singlehood, my goal was to find the woman of my dreams—the last love of my life. I had a clear goal, and I had every intention of reaching my goal to find my perfect partner. I also decided that I was going to enjoy my journey to find The One for me.

I made the conscious decision to learn how to attract love to my life. I began to write down the tips and strategies that worked for me. I also recorded the bits of advice that women and men shared with me about looking for love and keeping love alive. Little by little, I created a roadmap that consisted of a series of guidelines and advice about men, women, relationships, and love.

I now call these the Love Magnet Rules. When you follow these rules, you will attract love—just like a magnet attracts steel. If you keep using the Love Magnet Rules (especially those toward the end of the book), the loving relationship you have attracted and created will grow and become stronger.

How do I know this? I used the Love Magnet Rules to meet the woman of my dreams. We had a big wedding and a storybook honeymoon, and we are in the process of living happily ever after. Other singles, both female and male, have successfully followed these rules and are now in committed, loving relationships. But none of that would have been possible if we hadn't done the work and followed the Love Magnet Rules.

So this book is my way of sharing the many tips and kernels of wisdom I learned about men, women, and relationships. By learning the Love Magnet Rules and following these tips and guidelines, anyone (even a clueless guy like I used to be) can find, date, and keep the love of his or her dreams.

This book is written for both women and men. You'll find that every Love Magnet Rule speaks in its own way to both genders. You'll learn specific tips that will help you find and keep the lover who is right for you. You'll also get valuable insights into how the other sex thinks and behaves—and these insights will make you an even more powerful Love Magnet.

If you follow these rules, you *will* become a Love Magnet, and you *will* get your dream lover. It might not happen overnight, and it will take some effort on your part.

But it will happen.

Chad Stone
www.chadstone.us
chad@chadstone.us

Love Magnet Rule #1

To be a Love Magnet,
you must believe you are a Love Magnet.

You want to attract love into your life, right? The best way to do that is to become a Love Magnet. You need to become the kind of joyful, amazing woman that men picture when they think about love and commitment. Or, if you're a man, you need to become the kind of man that women are drawn to because of the strength of your character and your willingness to embrace true love.

In other words, you need to become a magnet for love.

The first step toward finding your perfect lover happens inside your head: you start thinking of yourself as a Love Magnet. Really. You need to open yourself to love and begin to think of yourself as a magnet that will attract love. And not just any love, because your Love Magnet frequency is uniquely your own, and when it becomes fine-tuned it will attract only the specific kind of love and lover that you want.

This might seem a little difficult for you at first. Maybe you've never read self-help books because you thought they were for dreamers. Perhaps you believe that positive thinking is a bunch of crap. Well, it's time to change your mind. (You *are* still single, right? Unless you want to stay single, you're going to have to do something differently.)

It's time for you to start thinking like an optimist. It's time for you to start believing that your perfect lover is out there waiting for you. It's time for you to start changing your mind about how love is going to come into your life. You have to start believing in your own ability to create the change you want to see in your life.

Belief is an amazing and powerful force. If you start thinking of yourself as a Love Magnet—and you begin to really believe it— you are going to start acting differently. You will begin to speak and act with more confidence, because confidence comes from believing in yourself. You will begin to relax and get in touch with the power that makes you both unique and appealing to the opposite sex.

Men are attracted to women who are happy and content with themselves. Men are intrigued when a woman doesn't *need* someone to love, but still embraces love. A woman like this is a true Love Magnet, and she attracts a strong man who knows how to love and please a woman.

Women love a confident man. Not cocky and arrogant, but quietly confident and self-assured. A man who is comfortable with his masculine energy without needing to flaunt it is the kind of man who has no trouble attracting interest from quality women.

If you can get comfortable with the idea of being a person who is confident, joyful, and self-fulfilled, then you are well on your way to becoming a Love Magnet. You are on your way to attracting and meeting the person who is the right love match for you.

Get a piece of paper or a three-by-five-inch card. Write **"I am a Love Magnet"** on the card, and put it where you will see it several times a day. That's your new affirmation. Read it out loud as often as you can. Hear yourself saying the words and let them sink into your brain. In your mind's eye, see yourself smiling and effortlessly talking to an attractive man or an intriguing woman. You are confident and desirable. You will attract the perfect lover into your life. Believe it.

With this small daily step, your journey to love begins. When you are ready, and when the time is right, you *will* find the right person to love.

Love Magnet Rule #2

Describe your perfect lover.

If you don't know what kind of person you're looking for, how will you know it when you find him or her?

After you have begun to think of yourself as a Love Magnet, you need to know what kind of person you want to attract.

Do you know exactly what your perfect lover looks like? Do you know what personality traits he or she has? What kind of relationship background does he or she have?

It's time for you to create a detailed picture of the person you want to attract to your life.

Get a pad of paper and sit down on the couch or in your most comfortable chair. Turn off the TV, your iPad, and your mobile phone. At the top of a blank page write **My Perfect Love.** Now start writing the physical appearance, personality traits, emotional attributes, and other details that best describe the perfect love partner for you. Make your list as detailed and complete as you can.

How old is this person?

What color is his hair?

What kind of work does she do?

Does he have any pets?

Where does she live?

Has he or she been previously married?

Does he or she have any kids?

How much money does he make?

How much education does she have?

How would you describe his or her character?

Does he have a sense of humor?

Is she a high-achieving Type A personality or a laid-back Type B?

Thinking about your new love will force you to think about what you *want* in a partner, what you *must* have in a partner and what you're *willing to be flexible* about. For example, are you willing to consider a long-distance relationship—at least for a while? Are you willing to consider someone of a different ethnic or religious background? As you write down what you are looking for, also think about your relationship deal breakers—the things you will *absolutely not* tolerate in a lover.

The great thing is this: there is no such thing as one single person who is the perfect love for everyone. Your sister's description of the perfect lover might be completely different from your description. She might like the cowboy type, and you might be attracted to fashionable urban men. She might like California blonds and you might like men who are dark and European.

It's important for you to be clear about what your perfect love looks like and how he or she behaves. But it's also important to realize that it's perfectly fine if your love doesn't match anyone else's idea of the perfect love.

I want to go on record as saying that you've got to treat people with dignity and respect if you're going to win the love of your dreams. You can't be a big jerk or an insensitive witch and expect the universe to present you with a flawless person as your lover. It doesn't work that way.

To be a successful Love Magnet, be the kindest, most loving, and most enlightened version of you that you can be. Be true to yourself—but be the very best version of you. If you're a man, relish the masculine energy that you bring to your dating life. That masculine energy is what women want, and that strong male energy will help attract your perfect love to you. If you're a woman, relish the feminine energy that makes you so delightfully attractive to a man.

After you've made your detailed list and thought about the lover that you are looking for, you'll have a clear idea of what you want. Hopefully, you have also made a commitment to be the best version of yourself as you begin your search for love. Now you're ready to begin the journey. So let's get started.

Love awaits.

Love Magnet Rule #3

Stop complaining about your love life. Right now.

Poor, poor, pitiful you. There is no love in your life—at least there is no lover. You haven't found The One—that one true love to whom you would commit your life in a heartbeat.

Look at that couple over there. They look so happy. Why do they deserve to be in love when I am not? What's the matter with me? I deserve to have love, but I just can't seem to find the right person.

Where, oh where is he? Why hasn't my Prince Charming found me yet? Oh, poor, poor, lonesome me. Maybe I should just lay down on my bed, alone in the dark, and cry until the tears roll into my ears.

Does that sound familiar? Does that sound like you? THEN STOP IT! RIGHT NOW. If that's the message that plays over and over in your head, then you are your worst enemy, and you are the reason you haven't found your lover.

You need to stop complaining about your love life. Immediately. Your love life is not going to change for the better as long as you continue to complain about it.

Many people think that complaining is a way to process feelings and identify what you do not want in your life. (In this case, that would be the absence of a lover.) Perhaps that's true, for about five minutes. But after five or ten minutes of complaining, it's time to move on. Complaining about not having a wonderful lover in your life does nothing to solve the problem. In fact, it brings more of the problem into your life. The longer you complain about how horrible it is that you are not yet in love with The One, the longer you keep The One from arriving in your life.

Instead of complaining about your love life, start envisioning the person you described in Love Magnet Rule #2. You know what you want. See him. Feel his energy. Know that he is looking for you, and when your heart is open—and not filled with complaints and disappointments, you will be ready for your lover to find you.

Love Magnet Rule #4

Love Magnets are always prepared for conversation and other love-related activities.

I was never a Boy Scout, but the Scouts nailed it with the whole "be prepared" thing. If you are going to be a Love Magnet, then you have to be ready.

"Ready for what?" you ask. Well, first, and most important, you need to be ready to interact with and talk with the opposite sex.

Men: when you catch a woman's eye at Starbucks, smile. When you hold a door open for an attractive woman and she gives you a smile, be ready to start a conversation.

Women: when you see a man checking you out, smile. A real man likes to make the first move, but a man doesn't like to approach a woman who looks like she won't be friendly and accessible. So use your eyes and your smile to tell him, "I would love for you to come over and say hello."

Build some extra time in your day to talk to friends, acquaintances, and strangers. If you have friends of the opposite sex, call them up and learn how to engage them in a friendly chat. Go to a coffee shop when you have a few extra minutes, and be open to the opportunity to start a conversation with a man or woman who you don't know. And by all means, chat with women and men who you do know—even if you just know them a little. That's how you get to know them better, and that's how you become an irresistible conversationalist.

Being easy to talk to, and being good at starting up a conversation at the spur of the moment, is an incredible tool to have in your Love Magnet portfolio. Virtually all great love relationships start with some great conversation.

There's one more thing about being prepared: be prepared for safe sex. It's the 21st century, and we all know about STDs (sexually transmitted diseases) and how to prevent them. So don't be an idiot. Buy condoms and use them.

One day, in the not-too-distant future when you have found your lover, you will be in a loving, monogamous relationship. That's when you won't need condoms for disease prevention. Until then, put a raincoat on your little friend.

Love Magnet Rule #5

Love Magnets don't sit at home all by themselves on Friday night.

You know why a lot of single men don't have girlfriends? They sit on their butts in their apartments playing video games, watching mindless shows on cable TV, or watching "epic fail" videos on YouTube. Their "girlfriends" are video screens and remote controls. They literally don't have time in their lives for a relationship with a wonderful woman because they waste so much of their time.

When you ask a couch-sitting man why he doesn't have a girlfriend, he'll tell you that there aren't any good women out there anymore. Like he's such an incredible catch, his hands covered with the slimy yellow-orange residue of the jumbo bag of Cheetos that he just ate.

Women do a similar thing. They sit alone at home or with their friends watching romantic comedies on Netflix or sappy movies on the Hallmark Channel while eating bowls of chocolate-chip cookie dough. They want so desperately for their Fairy Godmother to wave her magic wand and bring love to their lives. But unless the

Domino's Pizza delivery guy turns out to be Prince Charming, it just ain't gonna happen.

What's the solution? Get up and get out of the house. Go somewhere. Do something! Take your dog for a walk around the block. Go to the gym. Go out for a drink with your friends. Browse through the local health food store. Go to a lecture or a free event. It almost doesn't matter what you do, as long as you do something.

When I was single and looking for that one special woman to bring joy to my life, there were some Friday nights that I could have comfortably sat on my couch watching TV. Instead, I walked from my bachelor apartment to the nearby neighborhood pub, or I went somewhere else where I would have the opportunity to interact with people. I put myself in a situation that could lead to meeting the woman of my dreams.

Based on personal experience, I knew that the odds of a beautiful woman knocking unexpectedly on my front door were extremely slim. In fact, the only time I ever remember this happening was when an attractive Jehovah's Witness knocked on my door in an attempt to save my soul. Although this young lady was gorgeous, the random occurrence of her knocking on my door did not result in me going out with her.

That's why I got off the couch on Friday night and ventured out where I could meet women.

If you're a woman, I wouldn't advise you to go to a bar alone to meet men. But you and a girlfriend *can* go to a party or a club where there will be single men you can talk to.

Remember—you can't really be a Love Magnet if there aren't any potential lovers around.

Love Magnet Rule #6

Men make the first move, and women encourage them to do so.

It's the 21st century. We are living in the modern age of the Apple Watch and gender equality. Women serve in the Army, and they hold down important jobs in all industries. So why do the old-fashioned gender roles still apply to dating and mating?

Because it's encoded in our DNA. Ever since cavemen started seeking the company of cavewomen, men have been the hunters and women have been the object of the hunt. Modern men don't do nearly as much hunting as their cavemen ancestors—except when it's time to find a mate. When it's time to find a lover, the hunter instinct that's buried deep within us kicks in.

That, in a nutshell, is why men make the first move.

I know what some men say about this: "Why should I do all the work? Why do I have to be the one to walk all the way across a crowded bar to say hello? Why do I have to be the one to offer to buy the gorgeous woman a drink? Why do I have to be the one to risk rejection?"

Because women love it when a man makes the first move. That's why.

Sure, there are some women who find this old-fashioned approach to meeting and dating archaic. Women are used to being more proactive in their lives. They are bosses at work, and they are comfortable with giving orders and taking control.

But when it's time to go from business to romance, most women want to relax into those old-fashioned gender roles. Most women find it sexy and attractive when a man takes the initiative and seeks a woman out. It's a tremendous compliment to a woman when a man makes the first move.

Men: when you see an attractive woman at a restaurant, a party, at church, or anywhere, the chances are that she's not going to walk over to you and say hello. You're going to have to walk over and introduce yourself. So take a deep breath, put a smile on your face, go over there, and talk to her.

Women: what is your role in this mating behavior? Your job is to be so irresistible and so approachable that he *has* to talk to you.

How do you do that? With your smile and with your eye contact. Be bold enough to look him in the eyes for five full seconds. (One thousand, two thousand, three thousand, four thousand, five thousand.) Then look demurely away. Then look back at him. If he doesn't walk over to talk to you, he's a fool.

But ladies, you don't have to just sit there. You can employ some tactics to make it easier to approach you. If there's a guy you really want to meet, get up and walk past him—slowly. Get closer to him and give him a little smile as you go by. Or, if he's sitting next to you, ask him a question. Don't try to pick him up, because that's his job. Just do everything you can to get him motivated to talk to you.

If he doesn't respond, he's probably not worthy of you.

Love Magnet Rule #7

Always have your Love Radar activated, and always check out the possibilities.

You're out there in the world, living your life. Maybe you're standing line at the deli, waiting for a sandwich. The man in front of you is attractive, but you don't even notice him. Or you are dropping clothes off at the cleaners, and the woman behind the counter has a smile that could light up the night. Or you're at the gym working out, and a few people nearby are talking about a book that you are reading.

If you're not paying attention to what's going on around you, then you could be missing wonderful opportunities to meet the love of your life.

It's really quite simple to activate your Love Radar so you can notice people as you navigate your way through the everyday activities of your life. You hear stories all the time about how people met their husbands, wives, boyfriends, and girlfriends. Lots of these stories involve "chance" encounters that resulted in long-term relationships.

So start by paying attention. Be aware of the people who are standing in line in front of you or behind you.

Men: notice when a woman walks into a store just as you do. For goodness' sake, hold the door open for her, say hello, and give her a big smile.

Women: graciously let a man open the door for you. Get in the habit of saying hello to strangers.

When you are single, you need to keep your Love Radar activated. By being aware of the people who pass through your life, you're much more likely to meet someone who you could fall in love with one day.

Love Magnet Rule #8

Love Magnets look for love in all the right places.

This Love Magnet Rule might be from the "Duh File," but sometimes we need a refresher course in the obvious. You can't meet the lover of your dreams if you go to the wrong places.

Men: there's nothing wrong with going to a tractor pull, a monster truck rally, or a prostate health screening. But none of these events sound like places where you're going to meet single women.

Women: If you're looking for a manly man, however, you might want to consider going to a tractor pull, monster truck rally, or prostate health screening. (OK, forget about the prostate thing and go hang out at a sports bar.)

Go where the opposite sex goes. Sign up for an art class at the local continuing education center. If you're a member of a health club, go to an introductory spin class.

Back before I met the woman who is now my lovely wife, I went to a Pilates class with a woman I was dating. The room was packed with women. There were 38 women and two men. (I counted.) Lots of those women were fit and gorgeous. I filed that information away for future reference. Fortunately, I never had to use it. But men, now *you* can.

Even if you couldn't care less about Pilates, try going to a class. Even if you're the world's biggest Pilates class dweeb (as I was), you will still be surrounded by women. And trust me, you will get points (*lots* of points) for simply being there and giving the exercises a try.

Women can use this same principle. When you go out with a friend or two to meet men, go where the men are—happy hour at steakhouse restaurants, car shows, sushi bars, and the pro shop at the local golf course.

If you have friends of the opposite gender, ask them what they do for fun. They will be happy to tell you.

Then go there.

Love Magnet Rule #9

Love Magnets are not afraid to learn new tricks.
This includes learning the tricks of online dating.

When I was newly single, I didn't know anything about online dating. I had heard about a few of the most popular sites, such as match.com and cupid.com. But online dating didn't exist when I was single in my 20s, so I didn't have a clue about how I could successfully meet women online.

So I visited a few of the websites and I started to do some basic research. I read women's profiles to see what they said about themselves. I also paid close attention to their descriptions of what they were looking for in a man. I learned that women want to be loved by a man who they can trust and respect. They aren't looking for scumbags and players. They appreciate men who know how to date and woo a woman, and then they want the right man to commit to them in a loving relationship.

I also learned that physical attraction is important to women, but movie star handsomeness is not necessarily required. Most women want a man with a sense of humor, and they want a man who knows how to treat a woman like a lady.

While I was in my research mode, I also read the online profiles of men. Yes, I researched the competition. What I learned was that most men hadn't really paid attention to what women said they wanted. That made it much easier for me to stand out when I wrote my online profile.

The point is this: I wasn't afraid to learn something new. If there had been a tennis-loving woman who I wanted to get to know, I would have considered taking tennis lessons. If I had learned of a horse-riding club populated by gorgeous women, I might have bought myself a pair of boots and joined the club.

What can you learn that might give you a chance to meet a new love?

Have a question about dating and relationships? Visit www.chadstone.us for the latest tips and advice from Chad Stone.

Love Magnet Rule #10

First impressions matter—a lot. If the first impression of you is bad, there will be no second impression.

This advice applies equally to women and to men. It's for all of you macho men out there who think a woman should flock to you just because you have pure testosterone pumping through your veins. It's also for women who mistrust men, so you put your guard up when you meet men and refuse to give them a chance.

I learned the man's version of this Love Magnet Rule the hard way. Once, while I was hanging out at a local pub, I started talking to an attractive woman. Somehow, the topic of conversation switched to blue jeans. I commented that women's jeans were usually so tight that I didn't know how they got them on.

My new female friend was wearing a pair of skintight jeans, and I asked her to turn around so I could see how well they fit. "They look like they were spray-painted on your butt," I said, in my best attempt at an alpha male swagger. But instead of sounding like a manly man, I came off sounding like a total jerk. I did not leave with her phone number in the pocket of my jeans.

I have seen women do the female version of the same thing. Women like to hang out in pairs or small groups and tease men.

They pretend to be interested in meeting men, smiling at them and flirting. These alpha women act as if they want to be approached, oblivious to how much courage it takes for a man to walk up to strike up a conversation. When a brave man does venture forth to say hello, he is met with thinly veiled contempt. If he persists, he is sent away in shame, for no man is truly "worthy" to a woman who distrusts men and who doesn't really want to open herself up to a new relationship.

Bad manners are bad manners, no matter what form they take and which gender is behaving badly.

So if you truly want to be a Love Magnet and you are genuinely open to the possibility of new love in your life, be polite and use your manners. You'll be a better human being for it, and you'll be much more attractive to potential lovers.

By the way, this advice about creating positive first impressions also applies to your online dating encounters. Don't be one of those clueless singles whose initial emails to prospective dates mention body parts, sexual innuendo, the age at which you lost your virginity, or your bizarre fetishes. People are smart enough to know that if your first conversation (online or in person) is creepy, lewd, or condescending, then so are you.

Love Magnet Rule #11

Get comfortable with yourself and
good things will happen.

If you are truly going to be a Love Magnet, you'll need to start feeling comfortable in your own skin. Set aside a few minutes every day to appreciate yourself. You have a lot to offer a potential lover—especially now that you've gotten yourself out of the house and are out in the world interacting with people.

Remember Love Magnet Rule #1, and continue to think of yourself as a Love Magnet. Get those confident Love Magnet juices flowing.

When you feel good about yourself, you feel whole and complete. You don't need anyone else to "complete you." Being in this state of mind is the antithesis of neediness. Once you are completely comfortable with whom you are, where you are in your life, and what you bring to a new relationship, you'll discover how attractive you will be to the potential new loves that you meet.

It's ironic, but when you come across as being less needy, other people will want you to be part of their lives. When you get comfortable with yourself, good things will happen in your love life—and in your entire life.

Love Magnet Rule #12

A Love Magnet knows what he or she wants, and goes for it.

Women like men who are decisive. They like men who know what they want and aren't afraid to go for it.

If you are a man, then you know that wonderful moment when the sexual energy begins to flow between you and a woman. Maybe it's the end of your first or second date together, and you've had a really nice time. You have enjoyed each other's company and now the dominant thought in your brain is, *I really want to kiss this woman.*

But you've never kissed her before, and you suddenly start to wonder if *she* wants to kiss *you.* She certainly *seems* like she wants you to kiss her. She's holding her head slightly up toward yours, and she's gazing into your eyes.

Slowly, you start moving closer to her as your heartbeat booms inside your chest. Then you start to second-guess yourself and you chicken out. Damn! A wonderful opportunity has been lost.

You know what she was thinking right before you chickened out? Oh, my, he's going to kiss me! Yes! I've finally met a man who knows what he wants and knows how to read my signs. At last, a man who knows how to behave like a real man!

And then you lose your confidence and she thinks to herself, *Crap, not another wimp.*

When you feel the vibe from a woman that she wants to be kissed, then gently and slowly move in and kiss her. If she doesn't want you to kiss her, she will turn away in plenty of time to avoid your lips meeting hers.

Here's another mistake that some modern men make. They try to demonstrate their metrosexuality by asking a woman for her permission to kiss her. That way, there won't be any unpleasant surprises.

But asking for her permission takes all of the magic out of a first kiss. *She doesn't want you to ask for permission.* She wants you to be a man, make the first move with confidence, and give her a kiss that will make her panties wet with desire.

Women, have I described this situation correctly? When you want to be kissed, don't you want him to be a man and go for it?

Your role as a woman is to give him as many green lights as you can. Gaze longingly into his eyes. Touch him lightly on the arm to break the barrier of physical distance between you. As the moment gets closer, separate your lips slightly in anticipation. And stop talking. If he's a real man, he will fill the silence by kissing you.

Go for it—both of you.

Love Magnet Rule #13

Well-timed flattery, when used skillfully and in moderation, can sometimes help you find love.

Flattery has gotten a bad rap.

When did saying something nice about someone become a bad thing? Why is complimenting someone's physical appearance or what they are wearing (in a non-work environment) considered to be politically incorrect?

Sure, if you are deliberately insincere or excessive in your praise, you have crossed the line from paying someone a compliment to self-serving flattery. It's really a matter of motivation. Are you telling a man that his tight designer shirt shows off his sexy biceps because it's true, or because you want him to ask you out?

Or both?

Personally, I think paying a person a compliment is a wonderful thing. Most of us don't say enough nice things to the people we know and care about. We don't show our appreciation to the people around us, and we don't tell our friends, lovers, and family members how wonderful they are and how much they mean to us.

The world would be a better place if we were nicer and we said nice things to others.

So why not extend that to people you just met—or want to meet? What's wrong with a single woman telling a man he has a beautiful smile? What's the downside to a single man walking up to a single woman and telling her that he loves her earrings or her necklace?

I'm talking about giving out compliments *and really meaning them*. It doesn't matter if some people call that flattery. Let them.

Here's the key: give your compliments freely and without expecting anything in return. Say nice things for the sake of saying nice things. Most people will love and appreciate you for it—and they will treat you more kindly in return.

It's really a win-win.

Love Magnet Rule #14

Love Magnets are confident and sure of themselves.
Even if they have to fake it (at first).

Cool, collected, and confident. That's what women love in a man. They love a man who is sure of himself and confident enough to take the lead on a date and in a relationship. Women love men who are comfortable in their own skin and their own lives.

But what if you're not feeling confident quite yet? What do you do then? I'll tell you what to do: you fake it until you make it.

Just relax. Take a deep breath, and try not to let your nervousness show. Act cool, and don't let your nerves get to you. Act as if you are in control of the situation and you know exactly what you're doing. If you act cool and confident, pretty soon you will actually become cool and confident.

Practice makes perfect. That's the way it works.

Once when I was on a movie date with an attractive woman, I realized that if I were to behave like a confident man, I would start letting her know that I was thinking of her in an amorous way. The thought popped in my mind that I should just be bold and reach over and gently hold my date's hand.

When I was 16 years old, I would have thought about holding her hand for a *long time* before I ever made the move. I would have been a bundle of nerves, completely unsure of myself. But now I'm a more confident man, so I just reached over and took her hand in mine. With my other hand I gently stroked the inside of her forearm.

The physical skin-to-skin contact felt great, and without a word it communicated my romantic interest in her. My confident actions told her, "We are on a romantic date here. Get ready."

This is one of the most important Love Magnet Rules for men, because women are strongly attracted to confident male energy. But confidence is an important attribute for women to have too.

A confident woman is aware of her own value and what she offers to a man. She does not *need* a man to make her complete, she *wants* a man in her life. She is filled with love and wants to share her love with a special man.

A confident woman believes in love, and she is open to the possibility that a new love will come into her life. She hasn't shut her emotions down just because she might have been hurt in the past. She has learned from past relationships (good and bad), and she now offers a wiser and more experienced version of herself to a new lover.

A woman's confidence is different from a man's confidence, but it is just as appealing. A woman of confidence trusts her feelings and her instincts. She is not easily swayed by a man's swagger. She takes the time she needs to look into a man's heart so she can determine his true intentions.

When a woman is confident, she is not afraid to say "No." She knows what she wants—and what she does not want. She will gently but firmly say no, and she won't feel guilty about it.

Does a man find a confident woman appealing? Absolutely. A confident woman does not give her heart away quickly or easily, so a man must earn her love and affection. A man must work harder to win the love of a woman of self-confidence, and that makes him value her all the more.

When a confident man wins the heart of a confident woman, that's when magic happens.

Love Magnet Rule #15

Love Magnets take advantage of opportunities to talk with the opposite sex. Even unexpected opportunities. Especially unexpected opportunities.

The singles who get the most dates always seem to have time to talk to members of the opposite sex. These conversations can happen in the aisles of the supermarket, or in line at the bank, or *anywhere*.

Love Magnets make the time to talk to potential loves, even if they are in a hurry. Sometimes these conversations are quick and to the point. A few words are exchanged, both parties smile, and a phone number is passed. It can be that quick and that easy.

Back when I was single and living in an apartment complex, a woman named Katie lived a couple of doors down from me. I had tried to casually strike up conversations with her on several occasions, but I hadn't really succeeded.

One day, when I was returning from the onsite laundry room, I saw Katie out by the pool reading a book. I had planned a busy day of laundry and running errands, but I instantly changed my plans in favor of talking with Katie.

I walked over to the lounges and asked Katie if I could pull a chaise over to share her shady spot. She smiled and said, "Sure!" I noticed that she was reading *The Great Gatsby* by F. Scott Fitzgerald and taking notes on a lined pad. She seemed to be in a studious, not a talkative, mood.

During the next 15 minutes, I managed to coax studious Katie into a friendly conversation. We ended up talking long enough for me to get sunburned (when the spot of shade moved away from my lounge chair). But I didn't care about the sunburn; I cared about getting to know Katie.

By the end of the afternoon, I had asked Katie out on a date and she had said yes. I considered that to be time well spent. If I hadn't made time to talk to Katie, right then and there, I might have never gotten to know her. And if Katie hadn't changed her mind about reading her book, she never would have said "Yes!" when I asked her out.

So, the next time you strike up a casual conversation with a man or woman while you're both waiting for your coffees (or whatever), be open to the possibility of a pleasant conversation that could turn into a date with a new love.

Love Magnet Rule #16

A Love Magnet knows when to hold 'em,
knows when to fold 'em,
knows when to walk away, and
knows when to run like hell.

Some glorious dates are made in heaven. Everything clicks. The conversation flows. You lock eyes with your date, and you listen to every word. You're both witty and fun to be with. Even if it's your first date, it seems like you've known each other for years.

Some dates go pretty well, and the two of you have common interests and experiences. It's still too early to know if this is a match made in nirvana, but you and your date are hopeful. The connection you are making seems promising.

At the painful end of the spectrum, some dates are disasters right from the start. When you ask, "What's your favorite book of all time?" he replies, "I don't like to read." Or when you inquire about what he loves to do for fun, he says, "I work all the time. I don't have time to do anything fun."

You are tempted to ask if the date he is on right now feels like work, but you bite your tongue. It sure feels like work *to you*. Right at that moment, you aren't having any fun at all.

If a first date crashes and burns, let it go. Cut your losses and move on. If a second or third date reveals that a potential "love of your dreams" actually harbors one of the character flaws on your "deal breakers" list, move on.

Lots of newly single adults are lonely, and sometimes they are desperate for love and companionship. As a result, they can be too patient with dates who just are not right for them. Sometimes they act like *any* date is better than no date, so they keep going out with a person in the hope that things will develop between them.

But as they grow in wisdom and confidence, many of them realize that some dates are a complete waste of their time. This is especially true if they are looking for true love. Eventually, they realize it's a waste of time to go out with someone who they already know isn't The One for them.

Like Kenny Rogers said in his classic song, "The Gambler," "know when to hold 'em, know when to fold 'em."

And when a date turns into a disaster, run like hell.

Visit www.facebook.com/ChadStoneAuthor for fun tips about dating and relationships from Chad Stone.

Love Magnet Rule #17

Have a Date Escape Plan for
dates that go horribly wrong.

It would be nice if every date went well. But we already know that isn't going to happen. Some dates go so badly that you need outside help.

When a date goes horribly wrong, it's important to have an escape plan that will get you out as quickly as possible. This is especially true for women, because sometimes a bad date can get creepy to the point of being scary. That's when your Date Escape Plan comes in.

Before your date, talk to a friend and let her or him know when and where your date will take place. Then work out the details of the rescue plan. You might give your friend instructions to call or text you 30 minutes into the date to see how things are going. Do you need any help? Is it time to pull the plug on the date?

Another option is to have your friend standing by to take your call. In a typical Meet and Greet first date, you're in a restaurant, coffee house, or another safe, public place. If your date is going badly, simply excuse yourself, go to the safety of the restroom, and call or text your friend. Tell her to call you in 10 minutes when you're back at the table with your date.

Then take the call and announce to your date that a friend needs your help. Tell him she has a flat tire or she's locked herself out and needs your spare key. Stick to the cover story that the two of you have worked out ahead of time.

Apologize to your date. Don't be confrontational. Don't act guilty. But firmly let him know that you have to go.

He might figure out that you've put a Dating Escape Plan into effect. He might even be upset about it. But don't let him talk you out of leaving.

Trust your instincts, and leave.

Then call your friend to give her or him an update—and say thanks.

Love Magnet Rule #18

When talking to a potential new love for the first time, choose an interesting topic and try to keep the conversation light. Don't talk about politics, religion or ex-lovers. Especially ex-lovers.

We've all had a version of this experience: You're at a party, and you find yourself in a conversation with someone you've just met. You're having a great time, joking and talking and getting to know a little bit about this new person. The thought pops into your head that this person could be a potential new love. Then, he or she suddenly starts talking about politics, and you quickly learn the two of you have completely different political beliefs. Suddenly, you can't get away from your new "friend" fast enough.

Politics can do that to a conversation. So can religion. Stay away from those topics on a first date, and tread lightly on these topics during any early date while you're getting to know someone. Unless specific political or religious beliefs are on your "deal breakers" list, try not to jump into these topics too soon.

As bad as politics and religion are as first-conversation and first-date topics, there is an even worse topic: ex-spouses, ex-significant others, and ex-lovers of any kind. If you talk about your ex with bitterness and disdain, you are instantly less attractive. If you talk about a past relationship with pain in your voice, it's as though you're waving red flags and shouting, "I'm wounded! I'm not ready for a new relationship."

Let me tell you, that is *not* what you want to do on a first date.

Most women do not want to date wounded men. They want to date strong men who aren't carrying the baggage of their failed relationships. Most men don't want to date wounded women either. Men are not looking for women who are still emotionally attached to their ex-lovers—or who are still in emotional pain from a recent breakup.

When you're in "getting to know each other" mode, what you want to do is talk comfortably about light topics. Tell brief, fun stories about yourself and your experiences. Talk about things that you love and get you excited. That excitement is contagious, and your date will have a great time with you. And he or she will want to go out with you again.

That is what you want, right?

Love Magnet Rule #19

Don't switch loves in midstream.

Let's say you're at a big party—the kind with a live band or a DJ. You strike up a conversation with someone you find attractive, and there seems to be the beginning of a spark between you. It's still too early to know if there's a real connection, but you're hopeful.

You talk some more. The two of you dance, and you share a drink or two. The conversation keeps flowing. You're having a good time. Your potential love is having a good time. In fact, you seem to have *a lot* in common. The way things are going, you're going to end up with each other's phone numbers in your cell phones.

Then Potential Love #2 walks in and catches your eye. Great body. Gorgeous smile. A nice, sexy energy. You are definitely attracted to Potential Love #2. What do you do?

Many single people would find an excuse to dump Potential Love #1 and try to get to know Potential Love #2. But that's usually a mistake.

Why? Because you've already started to bond with Potential Love #1. You have used some of your best moves and conversation starters. There's the beginning of something between you that might be chemistry. You've invested some valuable party time, and there seems to be some mutual interest. This is no time to bail.

Chances are, the gorgeous Potential Love #2 is arriving with emotional baggage—or he's already in a relationship, or she has 17 cats, or *something*. You have no way to know. All you can see so far is some physical attractiveness.

But someone else's physical beauty is no reason to dump Potential Love #1, with whom you've started to bond. So show some character. Give him or her a chance before you rush off to meet someone else.

A love in the hand is worth several loves that you haven't even talked to yet.

Love Magnet Rule #20

Beware of barroom lighting. Really.

Have you ever met a man in a bar or a dark restaurant and gave him your phone number? Probably. Then he called you and set up a time to meet for coffee or for lunch, and when you arrived you almost didn't recognize him?

Some guys will tell you that every woman looks good at 2 a.m. through a pair of beer goggles. I've heard women say similar things about men. But sometimes it's just the bad lighting. Everyone is more attractive in dark, barroom lighting. We all look at least five years younger and probably a point or two higher on the classic 10-point rating scale of attractiveness.

The important corollary to this Love Magnet Rule is Love Magnet Rule #21:

Love Magnet Rule #21

Don't get too excited about
someone you just met in a bar.

If you've met someone who you think is a potential love, but you've only seen him or her in a dimly lit bar or in the dark of night, don't get all twitterpated quite yet. At least not until you've met him or her again in the bright of day—and you're totally sober.

Sure, he seemed handsome last night, and you really felt a connection. But it could have been the Sam Adams talking. Go on a lunch date with him before you start telling all your friends that you just met the lover of your dreams.

He *could be* the man of your dreams, but it's too early to make any big announcements on Facebook. She *could be* your one true love, but you don't want your friends to think you're a complete idiot when you've realized that she's not really all that special.

Love Magnet Rule #22

Be open to all opportunities to meet someone new.

A woman once gave me a great piece of dating advice: "Be open to everything. You never know when you might meet someone. If you are not open to meeting new people and having new experiences and adventures, you might miss an opportunity to meet the next love of your life."

You can meet people who become your friends. You can meet people who become your lovers. You might meet someone (male or female) who introduces you to someone else who could turn out to be The One.

That was such good advice that I immediately began to incorporate it into my single lifestyle. I went to lectures, book signings, and business mixers and conversed with the women I saw there. I made casual conversation at the health food store and at the public library. I renewed my fitness club membership, largely so I could get to know some of my fellow exercisers better. I once met a nice woman at the park when I was riding my bike.

The list of places and activities that offer opportunities to meet people and make friends is endless. You can take continuing education classes or group guitar lessons. You can volunteer for

Habitat for Humanity, at the local animal shelter, or for another charity. You can join a book club or a hiking group. Or you can join a new church (or get more involved in the one you're already attending), join a bowling league, or take dancing lessons.

Of course, getting yourself out there into the world of people is just the first step. You also need to actually talk to the people you encounter at these places and activities. Some of the later Love Magnet Rules will give you more advice about that.

One thing is crucial: it's important to open your mind to the possibility that you *will* meet a new love—and that meeting someone could happen anywhere.

So what are you waiting for? Make the effort, and go out there where your potential love is.

Love Magnet Rule #23

Get beyond surface appearances.

Let's say you're sitting in a busy coffee shop with your friend. You're at a table for four, so there are two empty seats. Then two men walk through the restaurant, looking for a place to sit. You and your girlfriend are smart enough and aware enough to ask them if they'd like to sit at your table. Man #1 and Man #2 look at each other, then they look at you and your friend, then they glance at each other again. An invisible signal passes between them.

"Sure, thanks," says Man #1. (He is the alpha male, the more confident of the two.)

Congratulations! You and your friend have just passed the "Well, They Don't Look Too Bad" test. Now it's time for a casual conversation with the two guys. Man #1 will probably start the conversation with a comment about how great the lattes are or how nice it is for you to share your table. The men will try to get you and your friend to chat with them.

If you're a normal woman, you might feel an attraction to Man #1 because he has taken the lead. He might even be the more attractive of the two. But this is a great opportunity to get past the obvious. If you're going to be a Love Magnet, your goal should be to attract the perfect love for you. While there is nothing wrong with falling in love with a man who is movie-star handsome, a love that will endure over time is a love that is based not simply on physical attractiveness. Personality, character, kindness, a sense of humor, chemistry, and many other non-physical attributes are a better foundation for a relationship than looks alone.

So, in a coffee shop situation or anywhere that you can spend some time talking to new potential loves, use the time to get past the surface appearances and try to get a glimpse into a man's heart and soul.

That's where your future love will be found.

Love Magnet Rule #24

Use technology to your advantage.
Cell phones, emails, message apps, and
text messages are a Love Magnet's best friends.

When my friend, Carol, got divorced, she immediately started dating with gusto. And by "dating with gusto," I mean she started dating more than one man. Quite quickly, she was casually seeing three different men, shuffling them throughout the week like a juggler at Ringling Bros. and Barnum & Bailey circus.

Carol admitted later that programming their numbers into her cell phone right away saved her from embarrassment on several occasions. Knowing who was calling before she answered the phone kept her from having a man call and say, "Hi! It's me!" and her not knowing which "me" he was referring to.

The technology that we have come to depend on is a marvelous thing when it works. And sometimes technology can be a Love Magnet's best friend.

When you meet someone at a party or social event, you're going to exchange phone numbers, right? Enter their name and number into your cell phone immediately. Not only will this ensure that you remember their name and won't lose the phone number, but this will also ensure that their name is conveniently displayed on your phone screen whenever they call. Then you can say, "Matthew, I was just thinking about you!" when he calls. And it will be almost completely true, because a few nanoseconds before you answer his call, seeing his name on your phone *really did* make you think of him.

"You were?" says Matthew, sounding pleased.

It works every time.

Another great way to use technology to win a new love's heart is to send text messages at unexpected times. "Hope you're having a great day" or "I'm looking forward to seeing you this weekend" sent via text are the kind of sweet messages that everyone loves.

But please don't use the accessibility and ease of technology to send lewd messages to a potential love. Refrain from sending messages such as "I was just thinking about your naked body!" or "I'm really horny—how about you?"

That's a *really bad* use of text messaging.

Love Magnet Rule #25

Practice your Love Magnet skills even when you are not trying to meet a new love. Some people call this "being friendly and easy to talk to."

Once you get the hang of being a good conversationalist and you can charm the pants off of . . . No, let me rephrase that. Once you become a charming and witty conversationalist and you are comfortable in a dating situation, you'll find yourself being able to converse with virtually anyone. That's a wonderful skill set to have in your arsenal, and you can use it in a wide variety of business and social settings.

I remember exactly where I was when I had the "aha!" moment that Love Magnet conversational skills weren't really any different from cocktail party conversational skills or "casual business event" conversational skills.

I was standing on the open-air deck of a hotel, surrounded by well-dressed, prosperous people who were in full networking mode. I had a cocktail in one hand and a pocketful of business cards in easy reach of the other hand. The weather was clear and gorgeous, and it was delightful to be basking in the late afternoon sun with a faint smell of ocean water in the air while working the event for potential new business.

That's when I realized networking at a business party wasn't really that much different from cruising a cocktail party in search of someone to date. Many of the same rules apply to networking for business and networking for pleasure. Be friendly. Don't be afraid to engage someone you don't know in a conversation. Look people in the eye when you meet them. Remember their names. Smile. Ask questions and listen carefully to the answers. Try to learn something. Talk about them more than you talk about yourself. Have business cards in your pocket that you can whip out at a moment's notice.

Almost immediately after I had this small epiphany, a man struck up a conversation with me and introduced me to an attractive woman.

"Chad Stone," I said, as I reached out my hand.

I almost chuckled to myself at how quickly I went into Love Magnet mode. But the woman loved it. My genuine friendliness and my interest in what she had to say made her feel at ease and welcome.

As I talked to her, I proved to myself that many of the Love Magnet skills and techniques can work in almost any social setting. Being a person who is fun and easy to talk to just might be the most valuable social skill a person can possess.

So practice your conversational skills whenever and wherever you can. Because being a Love Magnet means that you can be charming—even when you're not trying to be a Love Magnet.

Love Magnet Rule #26

When it comes to the gender roles of dating, don't be afraid to be old-fashioned.

In the modern world of the 21st century, gender roles have begun to blur. Men don't dominate society the way they used to. Women have gone through the Breast Revolution, during which they burned their bras and then decided that, with the help of surgery, they could have the breasts that they always wanted.

Then women benefitted from the Paycheck Revolution and went en masse into the work force. So here in the 21st century, which I like to call the Jetsons' Century (after the animated sitcom set in the future), men aren't always the primary breadwinners. Men and women are both expected to have careers.

Oh, there was that whole Sexual Revolution too, during which women decided they were entitled to have orgasms, and they could have sex just for the fun of it without the risk of getting pregnant.

In the course of all these modern revolutions, men have become less decisive and women have become more independent. It's simply not politically correct for a man to make all the decisions in the workplace, in politics, in relationships, and in most areas of modern life.

As a result, many men think that they should no longer take the leading role in the dating game, either. Men have become so politically correct that they don't know how to woo and win a woman anymore.

Meanwhile, women have gotten used to being proactive and going for what they want. So they no longer know how to hang back and let a man use his masculine energy to prove that he is worthy of a woman's love.

The original rules of dating were written a *long* time ago. Even though almost everything in society has changed, dating is still Old School. We're talking *really* Old School—as in the man is the boss of the whole process. The man brings the masculine energy to the dating process, so he makes the initial approach, he strikes up the conversation, he makes his interest known with body language and eye contact, he asks for her phone number, he calls her up, and he arranges the details of the date.

Yep, the man takes the lead in almost every aspect of dating.

So what is the woman's role? She's the prize worth winning. She is worthy of the effort it takes to win her attention and affections. She's the object of his desires, devotion, and sexual drive.

It sounds so retro. In some ways, it just sounds *wrong*. But deep down, most women love to be romanced. They love it when a man knows how to use his male energy and go after a woman that he finds attractive. There is something very primal about all this.

So be the man if you want to win the affections of a woman. And ladies, let him be the man. Make sure you let him know when he's doing the things that please you, because he really does want to please you.

Don't be afraid to be old-fashioned in your relationship. You'll both love it.

Love Magnet Rule #27

Embrace social opportunities where you are likely to be outnumbered by members of the opposite sex.

Let me tell you the story about how I starting taking yoga classes. Believe me, I didn't sign up for yoga because I was dying to put myself into excruciating positions that are illegal in 27 US states.

I did it for the chance to meet women.

Actually, it all started because of one woman. One day, I noticed a beautiful woman leaving the health club, and I struck up a conversation with her. She told me she had just been in the yoga class. I decided right then and there to attend the next yoga class.

When I mentioned yoga to a friend of mine, Carl, he told me a story about a guy he knows who took a yoga class when he was newly single. He was only mildly interested in yoga, but he heard that yoga classes were a great place to meet women. When he arrived at his first yoga class, it was him and 15 attractive women. He had his pick. The woman that he picked ended up becoming his wife.

That was a Love Magnet lesson if I ever heard one: Go Where the Potential Loves Are.

There are lots of places where women outnumber men. Pilates classes. Book club meetings. In the aisles of a Victoria's Secret store. At a health food store. At a Jane Austen book or film festival.

There are also plenty of places where men outnumber women. Go to a typical health club or gym and you will usually see more eligible men than women. Attend a craft beer tasting and you're likely to find more single men than women. You can go to a sports bar during a big game (even if you're not a big sports fan), and you are certain to meet men if you are friendly and open. Even better, go to an actual sporting event and strike up a conversation with the fans around you—most of which will be men.

The possibilities are only limited by your creativity and your willingness to venture out into the world.

So go where the potential loves are. But also remember that being in the presence of single members of the opposite sex is just the first step. You also have to get their attention, smile, flirt a little, and be willing to engage in pleasant conversation.

This is no time to chicken out.

Love Magnet Rule #28

Sometimes it's not what you say, it's the fact that you are willing to talk at all.

Most young men are on a quest to find the perfect opening line. They are forever searching for the one perfect thing to say to a woman that will make her think they are sexy, funny, desirable, and cool.

Over the years, you've probably heard some really good lines and some really bad lines. I've heard male Love Magnets strike up conversations with lines that instantly got a woman's attention. ("I need some relationship advice from a woman. May I ask you a question?") I've heard some well-rehearsed lines that were so obviously canned that they caused women to groan. ("Did it hurt? *Did what hurt?* Did it hurt when you fell from heaven?") And I've heard some good lines that got ruined by a really bad delivery.

When I was single and I became more comfortable in my Love Magnet skills, I discovered that the best line for me was, "Hi, my name is Chad." When I delivered that line with a genuine smile and a friendly squeeze of her hand, I could almost always get a few words of conversation from any woman. If the vibe was right, and I held her hand just a few seconds longer than normal for a handshake, I could quickly determine if she was intrigued with me. Then I'd launch into a story that might result in a conversation, a shared drink, and then a shared phone number.

For women, the art of starting a conversation is a little more delicate. Men are expected to be the ones who stride confidently over and get the conversation going. But that doesn't mean you have to sit around like a wallflower, waiting for reluctant men to *finally* get around to talking to you.

If it seems like a man you want to meet isn't going to take the initiative, then you have to gently get the ball rolling. The trick is to make it seem casual and effortless, like you're being friendly and not overtly trying to pick him up.

Besides saying "Hi!" and introducing yourself, the best opening lines for women are comments that flow naturally from the setting or situation you are in. If you're both watching a street performer juggling knives, make a comment about that. ("I hope he's got good health insurance!") If you are standing in a crowded bar, try something like, "So, why did you invite all these people here, anyway?" If you want to share a park bench with a man, ask him if you can share his sunshine. (Don't groan. Sometimes a corny line works great—especially if you give the hint of a smile when you deliver it.)

One secret about starting a conversation with a stranger is true for men and women alike: saying anything is almost always better than saying nothing. Women hate it when they catch a man's eye from across the room, they keep smiling at him and looking interested, and the guy never has the guts to come over and say hello. Men who don't get up the nerve to talk to a possible new love kick themselves for hours or days later. A woman who says something to which he can respond will find that he was desperate to talk to her, but he just didn't know how to get the conversation going.

Sometimes the first words out of your mouth don't matter at all. You could smile confidently and a bit mischievously and say, "I'll bet your favorite color is blue," because he's wearing a blue shirt, and that could be the beginning of a conversation that lasts for hours.

Most of the time it's not what you say, it's how you say it. And it's the fact that you had the confidence to say *something*.

Love Magnet Rule #29

Don't try so hard to become a Love Magnet.
Just be one—by being yourself.

Sometimes a Love Magnet in Training needs to take a cue from one of the masters. There's a funny-looking little green dwarf with pointed ears named Yoda who is known throughout the galaxy as a major Love Magnet. In the second Star Wars movie, *The Empire Strikes Back* (which is also known as *Star Wars Episode V*), Love Magnet Yoda said, "Do or do not . . . there is no try."

He was talking about transporting an object with your mind, but he could have been talking about dating and relationships.

That's because every Love Magnet knows that you can't really be a Love Magnet if you're trying too hard. It's only when you relax that you truly become irresistible to the opposite sex.

If you're like most people, there have been times in your life when you were single and available, but you were in a dating funk. You felt like you couldn't get a date no matter how hard you tried. It seemed like eligible potential loves ran away from you as if you were a zombie. And everyone knows that zombies don't get a lot of dates.

Sometimes, the harder you try to be a Love Magnet, the faster the potential loves run away from you. That's when you put on your fuzzy jammies and you watch something on cable TV. You put your dating life on hold. But if you are smart about it—even in the midst of a dating funk, you don't completely give up on your *desire* to find love and companionship.

Brittany, a woman who was in the middle of a dating funk, signed up for a continuing education class to get her mind off men—and off her nonexistent love life. She had always wanted to paint, and she thought it was the perfect time to explore this creative side of herself.

She relaxed and really started to get into painting. As soon as she did, she met a man in her painting class who shared her growing passion for art. They became friends, and then they started dating.

All she had to do was relax and stop trying so hard. It was then that love sat next to her in art class.

Check out Chad's blog at www.chadstone.us.

Love Magnet Rule #30

Be the first to arrive for a date—especially a first date. Give yourself a few minutes to claim the place as your own. This will give you extra confidence and help put you at ease.

In sports it's called the "home field advantage." Virtually every baseball, football, basketball, and other kind of sports team wins more games at home than on the road. And every host country in the Olympic Games wins about 50 percent more medals than they would have been expected to win if the games had been held anywhere else.

Why? Humans are simply more comfortable at home. We are more comfortable and at ease when we are in surroundings that we know.

If you're a man and you've put yourself in the manly role of asking a woman out and deciding where the date will take place, it's to your advantage to pick a place where you are familiar and comfortable. If you're a woman and he asks where you want to meet him, pick a restaurant, coffee shop, or another public place where you feel comfortable and at ease.

Even if you're meeting your date at a place that is not part of your "home turf," make it a point to arrive early. Check the place out and get a feel for the surroundings. If you're at a restaurant, coffee shop or a bar, try to get a table before your date arrives. If possible, get a table with a clear view of the door so you can see your date arrive.

Bingo. You've just given yourself the home field advantage.

Keep in mind that having the home field advantage won't magically make the date wonderful and perfect. But giving yourself a little boost in confidence might be all it takes for you to be relaxed and "in the zone" so you can make a great first impression.

It couldn't hurt, right?

Here's another tip: a large percentage of first dates now take place in coffee shops, such as Starbucks. They are safe, public places where women don't feel intimidated. "Laptops and lattes" shops are conveniently located, and every neighborhood has one because in the United States alone, there are more than 27 million Starbucks locations. Plus, a coffee shop offers a low-cost, businesslike approach to meeting someone.

Bonus Tip for Men: Want to stand out from your competition? You can impress a woman on your first date with her by buying her a meal. Ask her out for lunch, or really get her attention by asking her out for a nice dinner. You'll be sending her a powerful and positive message that you think she's worthy of a first date to remember.

Bonus Tip for Women: If a man asks you on a first date that involves a meal, he is trying to impress you. He should get extra points for that.

Love Magnet Rule #31

If you arrive after your date to the chosen rendezvous spot, smile and walk in like you own the place.

This is the second part to Love Magnet Rule #30. It might not be possible for you to arrive first for *every* date. Stuff happens, like traffic, work, and minor emergencies.

That's OK. If your date arrives at the designated spot before you do—even if you're running late, walk in like you own the place. Don't let the first words out of your mouth be an apology. Instead, give your date a big smile—and maybe a hug. Say, "It is so great to see you! I have been looking forward to seeing you all day." A heartfelt compliment is also a good idea, such as, "I really like that shirt—it looks great on you."

When his or her face lights up like fireworks, you'll know your tardiness has been forgiven.

Love Magnet Rule #32

Don't expect every date to be perfect.
Learn from the not-so-good dates and
try not to make the same mistakes again.

It would be awesome if every date went perfectly. It would be great if you were always charming and your date was always delightful. It would be wonderful if every first date led to a second date, and every second date led to a third date, because you both wanted to see each other again.

But life doesn't always work out that way. Some of your dates will probably even suck.

The way to become a Love Magnet is to learn from the bad dates. What worked? What didn't work at all? If you told a story about your childhood that was charming and funny, remember to include it in your dating repertoire. If the story you shared about a challenging time in your life turned out to be a real downer, remember *not* to tell that story on any future dates.

Going out on dates is a lot like going to job interviews. You can't expect to get every job for which you interview, and you can't expect every date to lead to a loving, long-term relationship.

But you can learn what works and doesn't work on a date, and you can learn to trust your instincts and be more selective about whom you go out with in the first place.

Learn from the bad dates—then forget about them and move forward. And *always* remember the magical ones.

Love Magnet Rule #33

Be careful what you post on Facebook.

Back in the olden days (before 2004), you needed to hire a private investigator to delve into someone's past. The investigator would follow that person around to see what he or she was up to—and maybe even dig through their trash to get some "dirt" on them. It was a time-consuming and expensive process.

Now there's Facebook, where our lives are posted for everyone to see. Like most things, this involves both good news and bad news.

The good news? We don't need photo albums anymore, because our lives are chronologically documented on Facebook. Want to know what you were doing in June 2013? You can go to your Facebook page and see the photos you posted. Want to know what your sister is up to now? She's posting every day on Facebook, so it's easy to follow the ups ("Here's the waffle I had for breakfast!") and downs ("Here's what's left of my garden after Buster got through digging everything up") of her life.

On the bad news side, Facebook can also be the repository of late-night rantings, political diatribes, and mean-spirited attacks on people who you know and celebrities you don't know. If you're really into sharing, Facebook can also be a vault of your inebriated shout-outs and photos with you and your friends doing things you should have been ashamed of the next morning when you sobered up.

If you're one of those people who freely shares everything on your mind, you might be surprised at what you have posted on Facebook over the years. And if you're one of those people who has an "open" page that lets everyone—not just your friends—see everything you've posted, then your life is literally an open Facebook page.

There are documented cases of people who *did not* get the job they applied for because of what the prospective employer saw posted on their Facebook page. (These cases include prospective police officers and others who should have known better.) There are also thousands of romances that were nipped in the bud because of what one person saw on another person's Facebook page.

Barbara, a single woman who always Googles her prospective dates and also looks at their Facebook pages, told me a story about a man she had met online. His profile looked good and so did his photos. So before agreeing to go out on a Meet and Greet with him, she checked out his Facebook page. OMG! The guy was a major weirdo, and he used his Facebook page for all kinds of political rantings and snarky comments about women—especially feminist women. Barbara is a liberal woman, and she was not amused. She refused to go out with him.

So if you're single and actively dating, take a look at what you've posted on Facebook for the past couple of years. Does it present you the way you want the world to see you? Or do your posts and photos present you in an unflattering way? Do you post too many pictures of food, pets, cute things, gross things, or your kids doing cute or gross things? If so, you might want to practice a bit more self-editing.

Most people share too much on Facebook, anyway.

Love Magnet Rule #34

Don't announce your breakup on Facebook before you've actually broken up.

While we're on the subject of Facebook, there are a couple more mistakes you don't want to make. Don't come home from a crummy date and vent about what a loser your date is. That's just mean and unnecessary.

Even worse is posting a relationship breakup *before* you have talked to your boyfriend or girlfriend and actually broken up.

Sure, you just had a fight.

Yes, you're upset.

Of course, you feel like venting your frustration and disappointment.

But a fight is not necessarily a breakup. Do you really want to tell your friends and family members your relationship is over? And what about your boyfriend or girlfriend? Do you want him or her to find out on Facebook that you've broken up?

I think not.

Love Magnet Rule #35

You don't have to be in control of every date.
Go with the flow.

One of the mistakes I made as a Love Magnet in Training was trying to be in control of every aspect of every date. I was on a mission to find the love of my life, and I wanted it to happen already. But a watched egg doesn't hatch, and a Love Magnet Wannabe doesn't attract new love if he's working so hard at being in control that he's breaking a sweat.

My attempts at talking to potential new loves were better received when I didn't feel the need to control the conversation. Most conversations have a natural ebb and flow, and often they flow wherever they want to go. Likewise, the best dates were those that flowed naturally when I got out of the way and enjoyed the process.

One of my favorite dates turned out to be a spur-of-the-moment walk alongside a riverbank in a local nature center. My date and I walked in the shade of enormous cottonwood trees and talked about our favorite places to commune with nature. Later, we spent more than an hour behind a bird blind, watching ducks and geese frolic in a secluded pond.

We counted turtles sunning themselves on logs, until we broke out in giggles because we couldn't tell which ones we had already counted. I hadn't done this kind of hanging out since I embarked on my quest to become a Love Magnet. Having a goal or a mission is a wonderful thing. But clearly, I had been taking it too far.

That particular afternoon date continued with an unplanned dinner, and then a trip to her house. We watched a movie on her couch—or at least we watched part of a movie. One thing led to another, and the date didn't end until the following morning. And it all happened because I finally learned how to go with the flow.

Love Magnet Rule #36

Pay attention to your partner's non-verbal cues when it comes time for seduction. Stop talking and listen to your bodies.

There is a gentle art to seduction. It's an art more than a science, so a Love Magnet has to constantly interpret cues from his or her new love to determine if the process is moving too fast or too slow.

In the vast majority of cases, it's the man who plays the role of the amorous aggressor. That's the masculine role, and any self-respecting man wants to be the one who initiates the first kiss. That's why he gently but purposefully reads the woman's cues and pushes the seduction forward.

How does a man know when to initiate further advances? How does he know when it is okay to move his hands from a strictly hugging position to begin caressing her neck, shoulders, and arms? How does he know when to go in for the kiss?

It's almost as if there's a Seduction Traffic Light that the woman controls. As long as she keeps the light green, a man knows he has her permission to proceed. Her "green light" signals include eye contact and an open body position. (Arms uncrossed, her face and torso turned toward him.) When she turns her head away, that's a red light. When she moans gently during a caress, that's a green light. Whenever she protests by telling him to slow down or stop, that's a major red light that can put an instant halt to the romantic festivities.

How can a woman encourage a man to go in for that magic first kiss? If he acts timid and unsure if he should kiss you, there are non-physical cues that you can give him that will serve as his green light.

Lean in closer to him ever so slightly. Lock eyes with him. Part your lips like you are starting the pre-kiss. Slowly move your face closer to him. Make it impossible for him *not* to kiss you.

That short distance between his lips and yours seems way bigger to him than to you. In that tiny distance you can reject him and send him home with his hopes dashed and his ego deflated. That's why men sometimes chicken out. They are deathly afraid of your rejection.

Give him every cue that you possibly can that he won't be rejected.

Inexperienced men, due to their own nervousness or lack of confidence, often break the mood by talking instead of seducing. But if you are giving him the green light signals—the soft smiles, the eye contact, the ever-closer movement toward him, the look on your face that says, "Please kiss me now"—then most men will get the message and kiss you

Let the romance begin.

Love Magnet Rule #37

Enjoy the rush of a new sexual relationship, because there is no telling how long that rush is going to last.

Everyone who has ever been in a relationship knows how good early-relationship sex is. But *why* is sex so good at the beginning of a relationship? Why do the sparks fly and you physically just can't seem to get enough of each other? How is it possible for sex to be so thrilling, so intense, and so frequent when you are in the throes of a new passion?

Well, for starters, there's the excitement of discovery. Everything with a new lover is, well, new. A new lover brings a freshness to every touch and to every expression of love. That touch can literally make your body tingle and feel more alive. The energy of attraction is palpable as it flows from you to your new lover and back again. There might be nothing quite as satisfying, in an utterly primal way, as being the object of your new lover's desire. The ego boost alone is a powerful aphrodisiac.

But what if the sex with your new lover *isn't* fabulous? What if you are not feeling the rush of passion and the butterflies in your stomach? Will the passion come later?

Perhaps it will happen. But more than likely it won't.

Valerie broke up with her boyfriend for that reason. There wasn't enough passion in the relationship, and she admitted that there was *never* enough passion in the relationship. In the beginning, that was all right because she appreciated this man's steady, even-tempered disposition, which was in major contrast to the crazy man she had previously been seeing. But, months later, she was dismayed when the passionate sex she was hoping for was never kindled. There simply wasn't enough fire in the relationship, so she decided it was time to move on. Fortunately, he felt the same way (for the same reasons), and they mutually decided to end their relationship.

So my advice is this: enjoy that rush of passion that launches a new relationship. Enjoy the hot sex while it lasts. It will naturally cool down over time.

But don't forget this: that hot, passionate flame can be kept burning if you both work at it. Stoke the fire by refusing to let complacency and boredom douse the flame. Light scented candles. Try a new kind of "personal lubricant." Keep going on date nights. Try a new position. Do whatever it takes to keep your love life hot and spicy.

Remember, too, that foreplay begins long before the two of you are in the bedroom. It begins with the way you treat each other, the tone of voice you use when you're talking to each other, the way you take care of your things, and the love and support that you show each other in a hundred little ways.

Begin to romance each other all throughout the day—long before your heads touch your pillows.

Love Magnet Rule #38

Any time you cook a meal for a lover or potential lover, you get relationship points. The more impressive the meal, the more points you get.

One of the oldest clichés about how to "catch" a single man is, "The way to a man's heart is through his stomach." In the 21st century, it works just as well when a man cooks a meal to impress a woman.

Why? Maybe it's because women have been feeding men for centuries, and shaking up old stereotypes by preparing food for a woman sends a powerful message in these ultra-modern times. Maybe when a man prepares a home-cooked meal for a woman, he is demonstrating that he can take care of her. Or maybe it's simply that women get hungry too.

Whether it's about the food, the nurturing, or both, cooking a meal is always a good investment in time and resources. The reward factor is high, and the benefits can be hands-on . . . if you catch my drift.

Cooking a meal for your new love and eating it together in the comfort of your home is a great way to move your relationship forward. Cooking is a profound form of caring for and nurturing someone you care about. Especially the first time, cooking sends a powerful message that you are literally welcoming them into your home and into your life.

If the dinner meal leads to a sleepover, then you can earn additional relationship points by making breakfast.

Love Magnet Rule #39

Don't jump into a relationship just because
you are lonely and the sex is good.

Yes, many of the Love Magnet Rules are about sex. (You're an adult, and you like to get laid, right?) But if sex is the only thing you have in common with a new lover, it's not going to be much of a relationship.

The whole "sex" thing is a double-edged sword. Psychologists and relationship experts tell us that most women fall in love before they want to have sex, but most men want to have sex in order to fall in love. So, men and women aren't on the same page at all when it comes to having sex—especially at the beginning of a relationship.

The physical act of lovemaking is fabulous. But it's only one component in a mature, loving, committed, multifaceted romantic partnership. If what you want is happiness, then make sure your relationship isn't just about the sex.

This might sound like the kind of Old School advice your grandmother might give you, but in this case old granny was right. It's often a mistake to rush into a sexual relationship. Without a foundation of mutual respect and understanding, it's not likely that a sex-based relationship is going to blossom into a romance that will last for years.

Yes, sex is an important part of a relationship, but it's not the only part.

Love Magnet Rule #40

Love Magnets are not afraid to learn something completely new. But they are also smart enough to take lessons, so they don't look like total fools.

This Love Magnet Rule came about when I decided to take a group dancing class. I knew that women liked to dance, and I knew that women liked men who liked to dance. I also knew that in order for a man to be a good dancer, he has to know what the hell he is doing on the dance floor.

One of the first things that the instructor told the class was, "In dancing, men are the leaders and women are the followers." That's just the way it is, because in a dancing couple, somebody has to lead. Maybe in 200 years the man and the woman will talk before they start to dance and decide which one is going to be the leader. But that's not the way it works today.

If you're a man and you're the leader, then you really have to know the dance steps. You have to be able to lead the woman through the steps and guide her across the dance floor. The only way to do that is to *really* know the steps so you can feel relaxed and confident.

Hence, the dancing class.

I found dancing classes to be quite enjoyable. Learning new dance steps was fun, because the man is required to hold the woman in proper dance position. While you are physically connected to a woman, you can't help but chat a little and get to know her. In a dancing class with 15 men and 15 women, partners are rotated frequently, so each man gets to dance with all 15 women. That's like 15 mini-dates, with dance lessons thrown in for free. (Did I tell you I love dancing classes?)

The women I met liked the dancing classes just as much as I did. They loved the safe environment, they loved learning the dance steps, and they loved the 15 mini-dates that each dancing class provided. There were almost always the same number of men and women at the classes, so it would be safe to say that both genders found them fun and beneficial.

But the idea of taking classes or lessons to learn something new is not limited to dancing. Take a paddle boarding class or sign up for zip-lining. Join a photography club or register for an art class. Join a gym and take as many of the group classes—yoga, Zumba, cardio fitness, spin, etc.—as you can. You'll have fun, you'll learn something new, and you might just meet a potential lover with whom you now share an interest.

Want to share a great (or horrible) dating experience, or get Chad's perspective on a dating or relationship challenge? Send him an email at chad@ChadStone.us.

Love Magnet Rule #41

Don't follow the "Three-Day Rule."

Somewhere in the history of dating, a supposedly smart man came up with the Three-Day Rule. It's a simple concept designed to make sure that a man never appears too eager when pursuing a woman that he recently met.

Let's say a man is at a party, he meets a lovely lady, and they have a great conversation. He gets her phone number and promises to call her. He really likes this woman and he would like to call her right away. But he doesn't because the Three-Day Rule says he should wait three days before making the call.

Why? Because waiting three days proves he's a manly man with lots of things going on in his life. He's not desperate, and when he gets around to it he might give her a call—if she's lucky.

It is quite obvious that a man came up with the Three-Day Rule because he thought it was a good way to appear strong and masculine. But when you ask women their opinion, you quickly learn that they *hate* the Three-Day Rule.

When a woman meets a man she likes well enough to give him her phone number, she wants him to call. But because of the accepted practices of modern dating, she can't call him—she has to wait for his call. And waiting for the call can be slow torture. She doesn't want to wait three days. She would much rather hear from him sooner. Maybe not later that same night, but soon—while he is still fresh on her mind.

That's exactly why a man should call her the next day. Tell her that you were delighted to meet her and you've been thinking of her ever since. Ask her out. She will be happy that you called, she will be flattered to be asked out, and she will say yes.

Even though women are not usually the ones who initiate contact during the early phases of dating, there is one contact that you should make. After he's taken you out on a date, let him know that you had a great time. Email or text him to say "Thanks!" and "I'm looking forward to seeing you again." A guy loves hearing that.

I'm sure I don't even have to tell women not to wait three days to let him know you enjoyed your date. You can send your message later that night or the next morning.

That whole Three-Day Rule is really a stupid idea.

Love Magnet Rule #42

Finding love is like buying a house.
Picking the right one is a matter of taste and
preferences, so don't take it personally
if you are rejected.

I love looking at houses. I enjoy having a Realtor drive me around town and show me lots of homes for sale. I once even had a crush on a Realtor who was trying to sell me a house, but I decided it would be better if I didn't ask her out.

One time when I was walking through a "fixer-upper," it occurred to me that in many ways shopping for a house was like shopping for a new love. These are just some of the similarities:

There are always lots of houses for sale, and lots of single people looking for love.

Not every house appeals to every buyer, just as not every man appeals to every woman.

Some houses (and some single people) are out of your price range.

Timing is everything. You can't buy a house if it's not on the market, and you shouldn't pursue someone if he or she is not single and emotionally available.

It helps to know what you are looking for in a house—and in a new love. As I looked at houses, I had a clear idea of how many bedrooms I wanted, what neighborhoods I was interested in, how much yard I wanted, how much I could afford to spend, and what condition I wanted the house to be in. Similarly, when I started the dating process I made a list of attributes I was looking for in the love of my life.

If you put yourself out there and actively look, you can find a great house—just as you can find the right romantic partner for you. But don't get discouraged if you don't get picked. It might be that the other person thinks your "living room" is too small or your "basement" is too big. You might think his "recreation area" is too small.

There's a lot of personal taste at work here. Just know that there is a buyer for every house and a perfect mate for every single person.

Love Magnet Rule #43

When you break up with someone (and you will have to break up with someone eventually), do it with integrity. Tell them face to face if you can, or at the very least on a telephone call. Love Magnets do not break up via email or text message.

Alas, not every man or woman you date is going to be boyfriend or girlfriend material. And not every boyfriend is going to be The One with whom you want to spend your whole life. That means, sooner or later, you will have to go through a breakup.

Sometimes a breakup is triggered by a bad experience (for example, someone gets drunk and behaves badly), or an argument escalates into full-scale nuclear war. But most of the time one or both participants in the romantic relationship know the breakup is coming for days, weeks, or even months.

The moment that you know a breakup is coming can happen at any time. You can realize it after a friend makes an insightful comment about the person you are seeing. It can happen while you are lying in bed, unable to sleep. It can happen after a bad or even a mediocre date. It can happen when the person you hoped was special has just stood you up for the last time. It can happen when you know he or she isn't The One, and you don't want to settle for anything less.

Nobody likes breakups. They suck big time, whether you are the dumper or the dumpee. Breakups can even be difficult when you are both ready to move on. But if you're going to act with integrity, and you know a breakup is coming, it's better to break someone's heart sooner rather than later. The longer a relationship goes on, the worse the breakup is going to be.

Don't be a chickenshit and break up by sending a text message. Breakup by text is the lowest form of dating and relationship behavior, and when you behave like that it gives you a bad reputation. Sure, it's easy, and you'll probably never have to talk to him again, but you will be acting like an asshole, and nobody likes an asshole. When your friends find out what you've done, they will kick your sorry butt. And believe me, your sorry butt will deserve to be kicked.

Don't breakup via email, either. That's also a chickenshit approach. Weenies (both male and female) breakup by sending "you're a really great person" emails. What a crock. If you were so great, they wouldn't be breaking up with you.

Yes, it is easier to break up via text and email. It's colder, more distant, and less confrontational. But a telephone conversation will give you and your breakee the chance to really talk and really communicate. In person is even better, especially if you've been dating for a while and there's a real relationship that's being broken up.

Look, I know you would rather send a thoughtful email than actually talk to the person you're been going out with. But suck it up and do it right. It's worth it in the long run. It will make you a better person, and that will make you a better Love Magnet.

I know you don't believe me right now, but trust me on this.

Love Magnet Rule #44

After a breakup, you need to get your own house in order—literally and metaphorically—before you can attract a worthy new love.

After a breakup, you might feel like crap. That's OK. You're supposed to feel like crap. It's temporary, and you will get over it.

Whether you're the dumper or the dumpee, now's the time to get yourself together and get your house in order. Take time to recover. Take stock of your life. Take a good long look in the mirror and forgive yourself. Give yourself a little slack.

Most important of all, give yourself some time to get your mojo back. Clean out your head. Clean up your apartment. Clean out your closet. Do all of the things you need to do to get ready for a new lover.

Don't panic. Take whatever amount of time you need to feel like a Love Magnet again. You won't attract the Love of Your Dreams if you're not ready. So don't force it. Potential new loves will smell your desperation and your woundedness, and they will run like hell.

When you're ready and your own house is in order, you'll find that a new love will arrive in your life.

Love Magnet Rule #45

Don't let your love-related activities jeopardize your relationship with your kids.

Being a single parent can be tricky and challenging. Sometimes your kids need so much of your love, attention, and support that there's no room left in your life for dating.

So there will be times when you have to put your dating life on hold—or at least on the back burner. Embrace these times as the gift that they are.

Spend more time with your kids. Go to the park. Go to sporting events. Watch family movies. Hang out together. Eat ice cream. Enjoy one another's company.

Your love life can wait for a little while. There will always be potential loves out there in Loveland. But your kids will only be young for a short time. If you don't take advantage of that window in time, it will be gone forever.

So remember to make your kids a priority. You won't regret it. Also remember to put yourself ahead of your dating life when you need to recharge your own batteries and spend some alone time. You can't give anything to a love relationship if you're so burned out that you have nothing left to give.

Love Magnet Rule #46

When you see a "festival of red flags," run!

We all have our own list of relationship red flags. These are the warning signs that signal something that we *do not* want in a love partner or in a loving relationship. If you see a red flag, pay attention to it—even if you'd rather not.

When I was single, I had one date that epitomized a "festival of red flags" for me. I had been taking evening dance classes at a local country and western bar as a nice midweek social event. It got me out of the house, and it gave me the chance to meet single women. During those classes, I got friendly with a woman named Elizabeth. She was attractive, had a great smile, and she was easy to talk to. Elizabeth acted interested in everything I had to say. (If you're a single woman who wants to meet men, this is exactly how you are supposed to behave.) I got up my courage and I asked her out. She accepted.

I picked her up for our first date, and things started well. We talked about dance classes, and we shared short versions of our personal life stories. There were some things about her past that were potential red flags for me. But I tried to ignore the warnings because I liked this woman, and I wanted to have a pleasant evening with her.

We had a nice dinner and split a bottle of red wine. Well, she drank most of the bottle and I had a glass. The more she drank, the louder she got. Red flag.

Then she started to ask me questions about telephones and telephone service. Not all at once, but scattered among talking about work, movies, and other topics, she'd say things like, "Are you happy with your current phone service provider?" and "How many long-distance phone calls do you make in a month?"

It turns out that she had signed up with a multilevel marketing company that tried to get people to switch their telephone service. I had the depressing thought that the only reason she agreed to go out with me was to try to sell me phone service. Another red flag.

Then the date *really* started to go bad. I found out that her ex-husband still paid all her expenses—and he also gave her an allowance. He also slept over at her house on occasion. "It's sort of a complicated relationship," she said.

By this time, I had lost track of the number of red flags I had seen.

Just when I thought it couldn't get any worse, she looked me in the eye and said, "Would you be willing to switch your current phone service if I could save you money?"

There were red flags waving at me everywhere I looked. I got the hell out of there, and I never talked to her again.

Love Magnet Rule #47

Get yourself a wingwoman (or a wingman) if you want to meet someone in a bar or nightclub.

It's difficult to go into a nightclub setting alone and successfully meet a potential new love. The odds are stacked against you. If you're a woman, you appear loose and desperate. If you're a man, you seem like a creepy loner.

That's why you need a wingwoman or a wingman.

The main job of your wingperson is to serve as the bridge between you and the person you want to meet. Let's say you spot an interesting man who is sitting with his male friend. Your wingwoman can mosey up to the guy, start a conversation, and warm him up. (She's the warm-up act.) Then she can say great things about you. When she introduces you to the guy, he already feels like he knows you and likes you.

If you're a man, there's something wonderful about hanging out with a wingwoman or female friends. It's like you've already got the Love Magnet Seal of Approval. If you're in the company of a woman, then other women automatically think you're OK. Women trust the opinions of other women—especially when it comes to men. So the presence of a woman is an unspoken endorsement that speaks louder than words.

If you're a woman, hanging out with a wingman or a mixed group of friends makes you seem more desirable. A man thinks, "She is really attractive and nice. I can see why that guy wants to be with her."

The great thing about having an opposite sex wingperson who is also single is that you can act as each other's "wingperson." Your friend strikes up a conversation with a potential love that you're interested in, brings you into the conversation, and then says something nice about you. Voila! Your wingperson has just done all the heavy lifting and you're now talking to a prospective new love.

There's also a group dynamic at work in your favor. Say you're with a few friends, especially if there's at least one member of the opposite sex in the group, and you're having fun. Notice how other people naturally notice you and want to join your group so they can have fun, too.

So bring your wingperson and/or friends whenever possible. You'll have more fun—whether or not you meet any potential new loves.

Love Magnet Rule #48

An ordinary opening line delivered with confidence and genuine charm is better than a really great one-liner delivered with creepiness.

This Love Magnet Rule starts out with advice for men. But women, be patient—because there's a lesson here for you too.

One of the most common questions that single men ask is, "What's the best pickup line when I am approaching a woman?" They're hoping to learn the perfect words to say to a woman they have never spoken to before. You know, something like:

"You are the most beautiful creature in the universe. If you go out with me, I promise to dedicate my entire life to your happiness."

But here's the catch. There is no such thing as the perfect opening line. There is no line that will work on any woman, anytime, anywhere. That's because most of what makes a great opening line isn't what is said, it's the delivery. It's *how* you say it. An ordinary opening line delivered with a smile is better than the world's best one-liner said with creepiness and/or no confidence.

It really doesn't matter what you say—as long as you're not being rude or crude. What women pick up on when you're trying to talk to them is your vibe. It's the way you own the space you're occupying. It's the way you stride up to her and have the chutzpah to strike up a conversation.

But you still want to know what the best opening line is, don't you? OK, here's a great tip. Men who are able to make a clever, offhand comment about what is happening at the moment (in the bar, restaurant, party, or wherever) come across as cool-dude Love Magnets. The first lines that sound fresh and unrehearsed always work the best.

But the very best opening line is the simplest one of all:

"Hi, my name is _____. What's your name?"

Ladies, even though you are not expected to have any opening lines (because the man is supposed to make the first move), you *can* take matters into your own hands. If there's a guy you want to talk to but he just won't make the first move, casually move next to him and introduce yourself.

"Hi. My name is _____."

That's it. You're still the female. He's still the male. It's his job to take over now and move the conversation forward. If he does, congratulations. He's doing what he's supposed to do if he's interested in you.

If he still doesn't talk to you, he's a weenie and he's not worth your time. It's as simple as that.

Read Chad's blog at www.ChadStone.us for more tips on dating and relationships.

Love Magnet Rule #49

It's difficult to attract a new love to your life if your life is already full. If you want to attract a date, make room in your schedule. If you want to attract a lover, make room in your bed. If you want to attract a live-in significant other, make room in your closet.

There's an old Buddhist saying that goes something like this: "The universe can't fill up your rice bowl if your bowl is already full." Yeah, I know that's pretty woo-woo, but there is truth in it. Now apply that wisdom to finding a lover. If you're trying to attract someone to your life, you need to have space in your life for him or her. Both literally *and* figuratively.

Your closet makes a great metaphor for your readiness to receive the Love of Your Dreams. If your closet is so full of clothes that you can barely get a pair of jeans out, then you've got no room in your life for a new love. Not only is your closet full, it's packed with lots of clothing that you're never going to wear again.

It's time to thin the herd, my friend. Get rid of all those flannel shirts from the 1990s. Get rid of all the funny-colored jeans. Get rid of all the pants you're never going to fit into no matter how badly you'd like to. Be brutal. If you haven't worn a piece of clothing for more than two years, get rid of it. If you can't even remember how long it's been since you wore a shirt, sweater, or a pair of pants, then definitely get rid of it.

Now you've got a big pile of clothes to give to a thrift store. Teenagers from all over town will thank you because now they can buy their Halloween costumes. "Hey look at me, I'm a grunge rocker."

OK, now there's space in your closet. Resist the urge to fill it with more stuff. Leave it empty! I know it's un-American to have an empty, gaping hole in your closet. But that's the space you've cleared for your new love.

Every time you see that empty space in your closet, tell yourself, "That's where the Love of my Life's clothes are going to be."

You're ready. Now go find your new love.

Love Magnet Rule #50

The man should always pay for the first date. And the second and third. A woman needs to feel adored and cherished, and paying for dates is one surefire way to communicate that to her.

To pay or not to pay, that is the question.

One hundred years ago, when a man asked a woman out for a Classic Coke—the only kind of Coke then available—he paid for it. There was no question. A woman would have been offended if he hadn't paid.

But what about today? When a man meets a woman at Starbucks for a Meet and Greet date, does he pay for her coffee and muffin?

Yes, he does. Being a single man who is actively dating can be expensive. But a man has to get used to it. Even though it's the 21st century and women have their own money, men are still paying for most of the dates. And that's especially true for daters old enough to have a divorce under their belts.

It's not about the money. It's about the masculine and feminine dynamic that happens during the dating ritual.

Dating is one of the most old-fashioned things we do. Most dating behavior is based on DNA programming and thousands of years of social behaviors. The courtship ritual is a complicated interaction between the masculine energy of the man and the feminine energy of the woman. Even though we're all thoroughly modern now and we'd like to think that men and women are completely equal, men and women still aren't completely *alike*.

The masculine energy takes the lead in the dating relationship. One of the ways a man takes the lead is by picking up the check. Yes, that's completely old-fashioned behavior. Modern, working women sometimes have a difficult time being taken out on an old-fashioned date. But for the vast majority of men and women, the magic that happens on a date happens more consistently when the man pays.

The man's job is to make the woman feel cherished and adored. What better way can a man let a woman know that she is cherished, adored, desired, appreciated, and worth impressing than by opening his wallet and buying her a fancy dinner or a night on the town? When a woman can relax and let a man spend his hard-earned money on her, she is actually giving him a gift. She is giving him a chance to feel like a man.

That's not to say that dating today is totally unchanged from previous centuries. Because most modern women do have their own incomes and they are sometimes uncomfortable when a man pays for *everything*, sometimes a modern man will accept a woman's offer to pay for dessert or coffee.

But men, don't let her pay for anything until you've got a real relationship starting. Keep that old-school, male-female dynamic going if you want to win her love. And women, be gracious when you accept his offer to pay. You mean the world to him. Let him prove it to you by taking you out.

Love Magnet Rule #51

Dates are like $100 bills. It's not smart to throw good ones after bad.

Unless you are completely new to dating, you already know that not every date you go out with will be The One.

Quite often, you'll need to go out on a few dates with someone to get to know them. As the dates unfold, you start to like each other. But it's still too soon to start planning a wedding.

I once dated a woman who played "hard to get." She did not openly reveal her emotions, and she was quite non-physical when it came to showing affection. She didn't even hug me until our third date. Then, when I went in for our first kiss, she gave me a "grandpa kiss." It was a little peck on the lips that a woman might give her grandpa.

There were things about this woman that I liked. She was beautiful. She had a good job. She had kids the same age as my kids. I made her laugh, and we had quite a lot in common.

But as she continued to play hard to get, I started noticing things about her that I did not like. She had an arrogant streak. She thought the world revolved around her, and it pissed her off when things didn't happen exactly her way. If she had a motto, it was "My way or no way."

I went out with this woman a dozen times during the course of two months. One evening, I called to see what she wanted to do over the weekend. She told me that I should take her out to her favorite expensive restaurant. But I was tired from a tough work week, and I didn't really feel like a fancy date. I told her I'd check my schedule and get back to her.

Until this point, I had been paying for our dates. (See Love Magnet Rule #50.) In fact, she had never offered to pay for anything. Ever. Yes, once she had cooked dinner for me at her place, but I had paid for every restaurant dinner, every movie, and everything else.

I had invested a lot—both financially and emotionally—into this budding relationship. But after hanging up the phone I realized that I wasn't getting a good return on my investment. In fact, I wasn't getting squat. I realized that I was done spending money on her. I also realized that there was no real chemistry between us, so I never called her again.

She never once called me, emailed me, or texted me to find out why she hadn't heard from me. And that confirmed my decision to not throw any more $100 bills her way. She wasn't the Love of My Dreams, so it was time to move on.

Sometimes women have to make the same decision. When they do, it's usually not about the money. It's about a lack of connection or an absence of chemistry. Whether you're a man or a woman, there might come a time when you realize the person you've been dating isn't The One.

At that point, it's a waste of your time to go out with them again, isn't it?

Love Magnet Rule #52

When scheduling a date with someone you think is or might be special, be as flexible as possible. If you don't have time in your schedule for him or her now, when will you?

Let's listen in on a typical call that a man makes to a woman to ask her out on a date.

Ring, ring, ring.

"Hello?"

"Hi, Valerie. This is Eric. We met the other night at the Britney Spears Karaoke Festival. Remember? We talked at the end of the event and I complimented you on that great blond wig that you were wearing."

Valerie is silent for five seconds while she scans her memory. (In Eric's mind, it seems like seven minutes.)

"Oh, hi!" she chirps. "Yes, I enjoyed talking to you."

"So, what's your schedule like next week?" Eric asks. "Can I take you out for coffee or lunch?"

Valerie is crazy busy. She's an attractive woman, she's popular, and she has a great job that keeps her busy. "The only time I can get together this week is for a drink after work on Thursday. Does that work for you?"

Eric had planned on catching a band at a local club with his buddies on Thursday. If he tells her he's got plans, she won't be able to see him until next week.

More great romances don't happen because of conflicts in schedules than for almost any reason—expect perhaps men chickening out and not saying hello in the first place. So what should Eric say?

"I would love to get together with you on Thursday."

Calling for a first date is no time to play hard to get. I'm not telling you to cancel a doctor's appointment or skip a class reunion. But if there's any flexibility in your schedule, use it.

The same principle also applies to women. If there's a man who wants to take you out, don't make it difficult for him. Do you *want* to go out with him? Is there a chance that he could be a quality man in your life? Then try to make your schedule flexible enough to fit him in.

If you've got a potential love's attention and he wants to go out with you, try to make that happen as soon as possible.

Love Magnet Rule #53

When you find someone special,
treat them like someone special.

Life is full of contrasts. That's the way it's supposed to be.

You will go out on some really bad dates with singles who simply aren't right for you. (Knowing that there are going to be bad dates in your single life makes these bad dates more tolerable.) You'll go on some decent dates, and some good dates too. It's important to know what a crappy date, a decent date, and a good date feels like. If you do, then you'll know right away when you meet a new love who gets your heart pumping and your blood flowing.

Because at some point, you will have a magical date with The One, the man or woman who is your perfect match. If you know how a bad date feels you will be able to appreciate the magic when it happens.

The human heart has a tremendous capacity for love. We all want to fall in love. We want to feel that rush of true love so badly that we will endure First Dates from Hell. We want to fall in love so badly that men will send out hundreds of messages on online dating sites hoping a really cute potential love will respond, and women will click through hundreds of winks and emails from men who clearly are not right for them. We will enter relationships that seem hopeful at the time, and then we endure breakups with lovers who didn't turn out to be The One after all. We will then start the whole dating process again, hoping that true love is waiting just a few more dates away.

All the pain and hassles of dating are the contrast that makes finding love so exhilarating. So when you find that special someone who makes your heart dance and your soul sing with joy, treat them like they *are* special.

Love, respect, defend, and appreciate him. And then love him some more. He is the reason you went out on all of those crummy dates.

Love Magnet Rule #54

If you can't impress the opposite sex with your classiness and sophistication, at least make them laugh.

If you ask women what they find attractive in a man, almost every one of them says "a good sense of humor." Yes, they want a good-looking man. But almost every woman also wants a man who can make them laugh. You know what else? Men say the same thing about women—sort of. Men love a woman with a sense of humor, especially if that means she laughs at his jokes.

I think the reason most of us find a good sense of humor attractive is actually quite simple. We all want to have a good time. We want to enjoy ourselves, and we want to find a partner who we can enjoy being with.

There is also something magical about humor, because laughing might just be the ultimate expression of comfort. A woman doesn't truly laugh unless she is feeling safe and comfortable, and *every* woman wants a man with whom she can feel safe and comfortable.

The most successful humor comes from telling an amusing story in a conversational manner, or making funny comments about what's happening around you. Being able to make people laugh is also a demonstration of your verbal skills, and both men and women appreciate that.

But don't try to be Ellen DeGeneres or Chris Rock if that's not who you are. Don't memorize a bunch of silly jokes, thinking that you'll have some "material" whenever you need it. When you try too hard to be funny, you usually aren't. Just relax and let it flow.

One way for even a not-very-funny person to be funny is to use emails, Facebook, and other social media tools to pass along little gestures of humorous affection—in the form of photos and jokes that can posted. That way, you don't have to be funny—you just have to be smart enough to recognize good humor when you see it.

Love Magnet Rule #55

Given the choice of talking about your last breakup or astrological signs on a first or second date,
go with the astrological signs.

There are some topics that you should never talk about on a first date. These off-limits topics include politics, religion, abortion, the death penalty, the infield fly rule, money, your last breakup, and any graphic stories about medical procedures or illness.

A first date is a time for light conversation and pleasant stories. Talk about the first time you swam in the ocean and got rolled by a wave. Talk about fun things from your past. Talk about your interests and your hobbies. Describe what makes you happy. Share all the wonderful qualities you're looking for in your next lover.

You can even talk about some recent dates that didn't go quite right. Just make sure the stories are light, non-threatening, and humorous.

Yes, the topics of your marital status and your last breakup might come up in the conversation. He or she might even ask you how long you've been single. Some of this is simply natural curiosity—and wanting to know if you're relationship worthy. If any of these topics come up, answer succinctly, without a lot of emotional angst, and divert the conversation to another subject.

The problem with talking about ex-spouses, politics, and other heavy subjects is that sometimes these subjects bring up painful memories and signs of emotional baggage. You don't want to sound like someone who is angry at every member of the opposite sex because your ex left you for the lead singer in an indie rock band. You don't want to sound wounded, angry, confused, or crazy in any way.

So stick to the safe, lightweight topics during the first and second dates. You'll have plenty of time to cover the tough stuff later, when you know each other a little better.

Love Magnet Rule #56

When a date asks how old you think they are,
underestimate. Better yet, say,
"I don't know, honey, but you look great."

There are some questions that you should never answer on a date. I call these the Impossible Questions. When a woman asks one of the Impossible Questions, it's a trap. If a man actually answers the question, he's caught in the trap, and it might be hours or even days until he can escape. Some men have gotten caught in an Impossible Question trap and were never seen again. An empty coffin was buried at their funeral.

The most famous Impossible Question from a woman is, "Do these jeans make my butt look big?" If a man says yes, he's screwed. End of story. If he says no, and she senses any hesitation at all, then she'll think he's lying. And he's still screwed.

See what I mean? Impossible.

Men have their own versions of the Impossible Questions that they sometimes ask women. For example, "Aren't cats great pets? If you could have as many cats as you wanted, how many would you have?" There are also Impossible Questions about a woman's past lovers, such as, "How old were you when you lost your virginity?" and "How many lovers do you think it takes to get good at sex?" Tread lightly, ladies. These questions are all traps.

Another Impossible Question is, "How old do you think I am?" A woman who asks a man this question is not looking for an honest answer, she's looking for a compliment.

So, how do you escape the trap of this particular Impossible Question? My favorite answer, which usually gets a positive response, is "I don't know, honey, but you sure look great!" It's flattery, but it's smart flattery.

There are other Impossible Questions, of course. You can never be prepared for all of them. But when it sounds like a man or woman has just asked you an Impossible Question, respond with a lighthearted compliment whenever you can.

It's your best hope.

Love Magnet Rule #57

Dating doesn't always go in a straight line. When your dating life zigs and zags, like the Dow Jones average, go with the ups and downs and keep believing that you will find the love of your life.

Sometimes you can predict the future. Sometimes you know things before they happen. Sometimes you get a feeling about something, and you push it out of your mind because it's not what you wanted.

A friend, Jennifer, had a premonition about a man she was dating. He was a desirable man, and she really liked him a lot. Jennifer sent him a friendly text to let him know she was looking forward to seeing him again. She got no reply, so a day later she sent another text. Still no reply. She heard a nagging little voice, warning her not to get her hopes up about him. But it was too late for that.

The next day, Jennifer received an email from the guy. It was a "Dear Jennifer" letter.

He dumped her. He had been thinking about her, and he decided that they weren't a good match. They were both busy and it didn't make sense for them to invest time in a relationship that wasn't going to work.

Jennifer had a sense that this was coming. She didn't want it to be true, but in her heart she already knew.

She wanted to call him, but she didn't. She wanted to talk to him so he'd change his mind. But she didn't want to sound desperate. She knew that men don't find desperate women attractive. She also knew that it only takes one person to break off a budding relationship.

When Jennifer told me this story, it hit me right away. Sometimes dating just isn't predictable. Sometimes it zigs and zags every which way, not making any sense at all. Just like stock prices. Sometimes men, women, and Wall Street make no sense whatsoever.

Jennifer only went out with this man four times. She realized it was way better to get dumped early in a relationship than later. But she still felt like crap.

So you know what she did? She took a week off. She spent some time with friends and she treated herself to a movie. Then she started looking for the Love of Her Dreams again. And when you get dumped unexpectedly, that's what you should do too.

Love Magnet Rule #58

Get a really good photo taken of yourself for your online dating profile. Use a "head and shoulders" shot as your primary photo so your prospective dates can see what you look like.

Let's talk about online dating. Sooner or later, you should give online dating a try because it really can work. There are millions of happy couples who met online, and most of them probably would not have met had it not been for online dating. But online dating has its own set of rules and guidelines, so let's use the next few Love Magnet Rules to offer some important tips.

The number one mistake that both men and women make online is posting a bad photo of themselves on their profiles.

The primary photo in your online dating profile is the first thing that someone sees when they do a search. Typically, a woman will search for a man within a certain age range and a certain distance from a target zip code. What pops up is a page of thumbnail photos. If your photo sucks, no one will click on it.

Or, if you're doing what you're supposed to do as a man, you search for women and then contact the ones who interest you. A woman then clicks on your email and sees a small thumbnail of your primary photo. If you look like a geek or a serial killer, you will never hear from anyone. Ever.

So here are some simple tips for a great online photo:

Use a "headshot" of just you. (*Do not* use a photo of you posed next to an ex-lover who has obviously been cropped out.)

Look straight into the camera and smile.

Get someone who knows how to use a camera to take the shot. It doesn't have to be a professional portrait. But the lighting has to be good so your entire face is clearly visible and not hidden in shadows.

Use a current photo. Don't use a 10-year-old shot, no matter how good it is.

Wear a normal blouse or shirt. Save your fabulous bikini or Speedo pics for later.

If you choose to add additional photos (and you should), please refrain from posing with your muscle car, your last boyfriend/girlfriend, your 12 cats, and your drunken friends. It's okay to post photos of you doing things you like, but don't overdo it. One shot of you at the beach in a swimsuit is acceptable, especially if you've got a great body. It's also acceptable to post *one* photo of you and your dog.

Here's one more photo tip. If your best friend is more attractive than you are, don't post a photo of the two of you. Remember to keep the focus on you!

Love Magnet Rule #59

Write a great online profile. Enlist the help of your friends to make sure your profile reveals the real you.

After your primary photo, the most important part of your online dating profile is what you say about yourself. The headline and the first paragraph need to capture you and your fun, charming, witty, and wonderful personality.

Your online dating profile is basically a sales brochure. The product you are selling is you. Most of us have never written a sales brochure before, and we've also never written anything about ourselves. When you sit down to describe yourself in words, you'll probably find it's a lot harder than you thought it would be.

Here's where your friends can help. Take one or two of your friends out for a drink or coffee, and ask them to help write a description of yourself that makes you sound wonderful.

Ask them these questions:

What do they like most about you?

What makes you a great friend?

What makes you fun to be with?

Can you be trusted to keep a secret?

Are you the kind of person who is quick to help a friend in need?

If your friends could change one thing about you, what would it be?

There are also many questions that you must ask yourself if your profile is going to do a good job of describing you.

What are your favorite things to do?

What are three things on your bucket list?

Would you rather vacation in the mountains or at the seashore?

What have you done recently for the first time?

What are you looking for in a new lover?

Why are you open to a new love now?

By answering all these questions and more—and by openly accepting the input of your friends, you'll get a good overview of the qualities, interests, skills, and experiences that make you a unique person. Plus, going through this process with your friends will probably be a lot of fun. And listening to what they say about you can be both enlightening and humbling.

Once you've gotten this input, simply pretend you're writing a letter to the Love of Your Life that describes the real you.

Because that's really what your online profile is.

Love Magnet Rule #60

Emphasize the positive in your online profile.
And never bash the opposite sex.

When I was single, one of my pet peeves was women who bashed their ex-husbands and ex-lovers in their online dating profiles. They would complain about how they had been mistreated by their ex-lovers, and sometimes that complaining would spill over to include basically all men. I remember reading those profiles and thinking, "Why in the world would I want to go out with you if you hate men?"

Sometimes the women I dated would tell me the same thing about men's profiles. Men would complain that their ex-wives and ex-girlfriends were crazy, and then they'd say, "Now I'm looking for a woman who isn't crazy. I hope that's you."

So apparently, both women and men can be totally stupid when writing their online profiles. Taking jabs at the opposite sex in your profile is just plain dumb, because that's exactly who you're supposed to appeal to if you ever want to go out on another date.

Your online dating "sales brochure" needs to be as positive as possible. No one wants to hear you rant, and no one wants to go out with a crabby woman or an unhappy man.

Instead of complaining, tell us the wonderful things about yourself. Tell us what you like to do—not what you hate to do. If you're a woman, talk about what you really like about men. If you find a man's biceps sexy, it's OK to admit it. If you appreciate the quiet strength of a man, mention that.

The old saying, "You catch more flies with honey than with vinegar" is true in online dating. Be the honey if you want to attract the attention of your perfect mate.

Love Magnet Rule #61

Don't be a lying, stinking jerk. Don't hide behind the anonymity of an online dating profile and tell lies to trusting, unsuspecting singles. Those who lie about themselves on dating sites will be cleaning toilets in the diarrhea ward of hell for all eternity.

I feel strongly about this. Can you tell? That's because people who tell lies in their online dating profiles are the scum of the earth.

Let me start with the men. There are a small percentage of men who think it's acceptable to tell blatant lies in their online profiles. These men lie about their intentions. They lie about their age and their income. The worst of the lot even lie about their marital status. Then, when they meet a woman in person, they will profess love, adoration, and their desire for a committed relationship. They do this because they know that this can be the quickest way into a woman's pants. Then, once they have "scored," these men disappear like 75 percent off sweaters at the mall the day after Christmas.

Men: don't be one of these lowlifes. Not only is it bad karma for you, but it's bad for the vast majority of men who are honest and decent. These jerks give the entire male gender a horrible reputation for being egocentric, manipulative, and only interested in one thing.

Women: you are not without some blame in this area. Some women also stretch the truth in their profiles. Women sometimes underestimate their age and their weight. Sometimes women jump into online dating before the emotional scars from their previous relationships have fully healed, yet they pretend to be ready for a relationship. Women tend to tell fewer outright lies than men, but sometimes their lies of omission can be just as misleading and just as damaging.

So let's all make a pact right now. Let's all promise to tell the truth in our online dating profiles. Let's bring honesty, civility, and truth to cyberdating. There is no reason that the online dating world has to be like the Wild, Wild West. We can do better than that.

Integrity begins with you. Tell the truth about yourself, and accept nothing less than the truth from everyone you interact with—both online and in the real world. We don't have to put up with the crap from the minority who hides in the shadows. If someone does you wrong online, report them.

You're looking for the Love of Your Life. It's all right if your standards are high. In fact, your standards are *supposed* to be high. You must expect the best in others before they will reveal their best to you.

Love Magnet Rule #62

Beware of blind dates, especially if physical appearance is important to you. Get a photo of your date before your meet to avoid wasting your valuable time.

You know why blind dates get such a bad rap? Because humans are visual creatures and a large percentage of what attracts us to another person is physical appearance. This is especially true for men. And even though women have a much more forgiving sense of what constitutes physical attractiveness, women are also looking for good looks.

No woman wants to go out with the Hunchback of Notre Dame, and no man wants to go out with the Hunchback of Notre Dame's ugly sister.

The whole visual attraction thing is one area in which online dating sites get it right. Match.com and all the rest figured out right from the start that they better encourage their members to post profile photos of themselves, and they better show you those photos right away when you do a search. Apps such as Tinder are even more visual, because Tinder forces you to make a "yes or no" decision about someone based only on a photo.

Clearly, we want to see our dates before we go out with them.

Most single people quickly learn the "no blind dates" rule. Julie had a "no blind dates" rule, but she let it slide for a man named Jeff who claimed he lost his smart phone so he couldn't send her a picture. They exchanged a couple of emails and then talked on the phone a couple of times. Jeff never got around to sending a photo, but Julie agreed to meet him anyway. She had no idea what Jeff looked like, but she liked the way he sounded.

When Julie arrived for their Meet and Greet date at a local coffee house, she immediately gave Jeff a 4 on the 10-point attractiveness scale. He was out of shape, and he dressed like a slob. He had a mustard stain on his shirt and hair that looked like a hornet's nest. Normally, she wasn't that concerned with looks, but the way Jeff looked totally turned her off.

In his defense, he was a kindhearted man who volunteered at the local animal shelter and seemed like a good guy. But bless his heart (as they say in the South), Jeff was not what Julie was looking for.

She knew after two minutes of talking to him that there was no point in seeing him again. And that was the last time she ever went on a blind date.

Subscribe to Chad Stone's free dating and relationships enewsletter. Just visit www.chadstone.us to sign up.

Love Magnet Rule #63

If a man doesn't make any post-date contact,
he doesn't want to go out with you again. Period.

He didn't lose your phone number. He didn't forget to call. If you don't hear from a man after a date, it's because he doesn't want to go out with you again.

Sorry to be so blunt, but that's the truth. You could be the biggest Love Magnet in town, and still not every man is going to love you.

You know why men don't call? Because they absolutely hate making that horrible "I don't want to go out with you again" phone call. Most men don't do things that they don't want to do. In fact, they do everything they can to avoid them.

In some ways, making the "I don't want to go out with you again" phone call or sending a "thanks, but no thanks" email to a woman is like deliberately contacting a woman so you can slam the door in her face. Even men who are total jerks don't like to do that.

So men avoid making the call, sending the email, or even sending a text. Yes, they use the Chickenshit Way of nipping the relationship in the bud. Men who have been dating for a while have learned that when they invoke the Chickenshit Way of not pursuing a woman, the chances are good that she will never call or email to find out why she never heard from them again.

The women's version of the Chickenshit Way is slightly gentler but just as passive-aggressive. Women simply don't answer the phone or respond to his emails or texts. It turns out that none of us really wants to be the bearers of bad news.

So, if you stop hearing from him (or her), don't go into a funk about it. Pick yourself up and move on. Get your Love Magnet juices flowing again so you can find the person with whom you're really supposed to fall in love.

Love Magnet Rule #64

If there are absolutely no sparks during the first date, don't bother to ask for a second date—unless you want a brother-sister relationship.

Have you ever met someone who "should" have been a perfect match for you? If the two of you discover each other online, his profile sounds great to you, and yours sounds great to him. He seems like what you've been looking for. In his online photos he's cute—with an attractive face and the right body type for you. Even his hair color is your favorite. Beyond his perfect appearance, he likes the same things you do. He even has a great sense of humor and likes the same restaurants, movies, books, and music that you do.

Your early forays into email correspondence go well. Even your first phone calls reveal what promises to be a real relationship. You have high hopes for each other. You might have even Googled each other.

A mutual friend would probably say, "You are perfect for each other." You can't wait to meet him.

Then you meet for your first date, and absolutely nothing happens. There are no fireworks. There aren't even any sparks. What happened?

What happened was there was no chemistry between you. Even though you've got *so much* in common, your personalities didn't click, your energy wasn't compatible, or *something.* Maybe he didn't laugh at your jokes. Maybe he didn't take much interest in your job—a job that you happen to love. Maybe you came across as a little nervous or uptight. Or maybe you got along pretty well, but there just wasn't any spark of passion between you. You just didn't connect *in that way*.

What should you do? If you're looking for passion, move on. Unless you want to cultivate a relationship that's strictly friendship, keep looking. If the spark isn't there, the best you can hope for is to be friends. Now, there is nothing wrong with having friends. Plenty of people will say that you can't have too many friends.

But you're dating in the hopes of finding a romantic partner, right? So give your new friend a warm handshake in the parking lot or a sisterly hug and keep looking for that special someone who really turns you on.

Love Magnet Rule #65

Trust your instincts. If your gut tells you the person you've been seeing is not The One—listen.

Even when you've met someone you really like—someone who makes you smile and sometimes warms your loins—that doesn't mean that he or she is The One.

Imagine meeting a wonderful man at a party who is hot and attractive. He was born in another country, and he has lived all over the world. He speaks with a delightful accent, and just hearing him talk makes your body tingle. You're delighted that he will even talk with you.

He is so exotic, so worldly! You drink him in—his rugged good looks and his foreign sophistication. There are other women at the party who want to talk to him, but for some reason he has found you interesting. He is lavishing his attention on you, and that makes him even more attractive. You give him your phone number and hope that he will call.

He calls the next day, and you set up a dinner date. He takes you to a fine restaurant and the wine flows. You can't believe that a man like this is still single. You feel like the luckiest woman on Earth.

During the course of a few dates, you learn everything you can about him. His life is so interesting. He's a free spirit, and he's done so many things. You love his energy and willingness to try new things. At some point during one of your dates, you realize how boring your life is compared to his. You are still amazed that he is willing to go out with you. He is out of your league, or at least out of your normal comfort zone, but somehow he doesn't seem to think so.

Holy Exotic Love! Sometimes you have trouble coming up with things to talk about that don't sound lame. You make a silent promise to yourself to get out more and get out of your rut.

You are smitten. You love his wild hairstyle, his European clothes, and his smoldering passion. But at the same time, every date reveals just how differently you live your lives. Maybe there's a passionate spark between you. Maybe the sex is great. But that doesn't keep you from noticing the nagging feeling that tells you he is not The One for you. He is wonderful, he intrigues you in a way that no one ever has, but in your heart, you know he's not The One.

At some point, you'll have to face the facts. You'll have to gently let him go. There is nothing wrong with enjoying this moment in time with him, and learning what you can from his pure, free spirit.

Just know that you both must eventually move on if you're going to find the person who is truly your soul mate.

Love Magnet Rule #66

Don't try so hard to impress a prospective new love with witty banter and death-defying stunts of bravery.
The best dates are those that are effortless.

When I was single, I got really good at meeting a woman for a date and being thoroughly charming. I could turn on the charm like it was a light switch. I had several stories that I could tell that demonstrated my wit and wisdom. I knew exactly what to say to impress a woman with my heart of gold, and I knew how to hint at my sexuality without being threatening.

If I have to say so myself, I was the Master of the First Date.

The trouble was, so many of my first dates were *exhausting*. I was trying so hard to be fun, funny, entertaining, and appealing that it was wearing me out. A Meet and Greet date felt like I was going onstage for an evening's worth of standup comedy and storytelling. I had enough material for 90 minutes. During the date, my adrenaline flowed and I was "on."

After a date, I would come home and park myself in front of the TV where I would quickly fall asleep.

Then I learned how to relax. I didn't have to be "on" all the time. I could still weave my stories and funny anecdotes into the conversation, but I didn't have to treat each date like it was an appearance on *The Daily Show*. And that's when I *really* got good at dating.

When I didn't try so hard to impress someone, I found that I was making a better impression and a better connection. I also discovered that I was getting to know my dates a whole lot better. You can't get to know someone else if you do all the talking. And even though women are famous for their love of conversation, they don't appreciate it when a man dominates the conversation and doesn't let it flow back and forth.

When I relaxed into dating, I continued to tell some of my favorite stories about myself. I still had fun sharing stories about dates that hadn't gone well. Not in a mean-spirited way, but in a good-natured way. Sharing dating stories is always a topic that generates interest among actively dating singles.

But I stopped trying so hard. Eventually, I let the elusive butterfly of love land on me, instead of racing to capture it and wrestle it to the ground. And that made all the difference.

Love Magnet Rule #67

In baseball and in dating, three strikes and you're out.

Let's say you're a man who has met a potential new love, and you've asked her out. You're looking forward to your date, and you're feeling like a successful Love Magnet.

Then, on the morning of your date, she calls to tell you she's sick. She really sounds sick, not like the "calling in sick to work" thing where you make your voice sound really tired and hoarse so the person on the other end will know how horrible you feel and there's just *no way* you can come in today. She sounds sick, and you're pretty sure it's for real.

"I am so sorry," she croaks. "Can we reschedule?"

So you do. Then, a week later, you get the same phone call. She still sounds all croaky, like a frog that got run over by a car. "I wasn't able to take any time off this week, so I need the weekend to just take it easy. Can we go see a movie next week instead?"

A week later it's déjà vu all over again. The woman cancels for the third week in a row. Sure, she still sounds sick. But enough is enough.

You had high hopes for this woman. But the stars seem to be against you. The universe is trying to tell you something. Or perhaps she is trying to tell you that she's not interested, and she doesn't have the guts or the decency to tell you straight out.

Either way, three strikes and you're out.

The same thing goes for a man who keeps cancelling dates with a woman. If he does that three times, he's out. Send him back to the dugout and bring in a new batter.

Life is too short to deal with this kind of rudeness, this kind of rejection. Even more important: what would it say about you if you put up with it?

Love Magnet Rule #68

Don't bother chasing singles who don't want to be caught.

Why is it that some single people are willing to go out on dates, but aren't really looking for a relationship? Why even go through the motions? What's up with that?

Why would anyone go through the trouble of filling out an online profile on PlentyofFish.com, or answering the 17,000 questions on eHarmony.com, and then not be serious about finding a romantic partner?

I don't have the answers to these questions, because it makes no sense to me. When I was dating, I was on a mission to find love. I didn't want to waste my time or anyone else's. I put myself online for a reason, and I was serious about dating. (By that I mean I took dating seriously; but I also enjoyed the process.)

But that doesn't seem to be true for everyone. Some singles seem to be going through the dating motions. Some even act like dating is their chosen form of entertainment. They go out on dates without ever getting even close to anything that resembles a relationship or a commitment of any kind.

If you're a woman who is honestly and genuinely looking for the Love of Your Life, then it's frustrating to meet a man to whom you are attracted, but he isn't taking dating as seriously as you are. You can waste a lot of time on a man who doesn't really want to get "caught."

You'll recognize a man who isn't looking for a real relationship by the way he disappears between dates and doesn't stay in contact with emails or texts. You have to keep your schedule open because you never know when he will call—and then it is usually for a booty call. He regularly finds reasons why you can't get together. Sometimes he cancels dates, and sometimes he's just not available for a week or two.

Beware. If you're looking for a relationship—a committed, stable, loving relationship, you are probably wasting your time, and you should move on.

Love Magnet Rule #69

The chemistry of attraction happens in person, and it usually happens quickly. When it does, pay attention to it.

The truth of this Love Magnet Rule hit me the night I participated in a speed-dating event. When the starting bell went off—yes, there actually was a starting bell—I was engulfed in a tsunami of estrogen and testosterone as 13 women and 13 men simultaneously launched into first dates. These were first dates on speed, so the noise in the room reached the decibel level equivalent to a NASCAR race or the front row of an AC/DC concert.

Among the 13 women that I had first dates with that night was a woman who, on paper, was a perfect match for me. We worked in the same industry. We had the same hobbies and interests. She was attractive. She was the right height and body type for me. She was happy with her career, but at the same time she wasn't married to it. She genuinely wanted to find a man and build a relationship that would last for years—maybe forever.

But of my 13 first dates that night, this woman was my *least* favorite. She was hard to talk to—and I can talk to anyone. She was sarcastic and hard to please. She didn't have anything nice to say about anyone or anything. Our date was the longest six minutes of my life.

On the other end of the spectrum was my first date with Krista. We had originally met online, and then our initial phone calls seemed very promising. And when we first met in person, the chemistry happened the moment I looked into her eyes.

I loved everything about her—but mostly I was swept away by the energy that passed between us. We were connected in a way that is difficult to describe, and it felt like we had met each other in previous lives. Or something equally as cosmic.

It didn't take long for us to fall in love with each other. We are now happily married, and the chemistry that we felt on our first date has continued to grow stronger—because we work at making it stronger.

Trust me, you need to pay attention when chemistry happens.

Love Magnet Rule #70

There's nothing wrong with a traditional Meet and Greet date. But don't be afraid to try something quirky and creative. And don't underestimate the value of an expensive dinner at a classy restaurant on Saturday night.

It seems like everyone's first date of choice is a Meet and Greet at a coffeehouse. It's a safe public place, so women like it. It's a cheap date, so men like it. It's easy to get in and out, so busy people of both genders like it. It's not a major commitment, the lighting is good, and the coffee is good too.

There's nothing wrong with a Meet and Greet at Starbucks. In fact, one reason it's so popular is it does get the job done. Two people meet each other for the first time, and they decide if they want to see each other again.

But gentlemen, there's also another alternative that will set you apart from the other boring guys your date has gone out with. Try something fun, something creative, something quirky. If the weather is nice, meet her at an ice cream store. Buy two ice cream cones (or low-fat frozen yogurt) and walk around the park as you talk. Rent bikes and ride around a fun part of town. Or how about a date at an amusement park—or a classic picnic in the park? There is no limit to the number of creative and quirky date ideas.

You know what really works if you want to get a woman's attention? Take her on a first date to a fancy restaurant. I'm talking white tablecloths, waiters who wear ties, expensive wine uncorked at your table—the whole works. A real, old-fashioned fancy Saturday night dinner date.

Yes, a fancy dinner date will set you back a few bucks. OK, more than a few bucks. But there's no better way to make a woman feel special, important, and *desired*. If you want to get her attention, this will do it.

And it works even better now because so many men have completely lost the romantic touch. You can bring old-fashioned romance back in style, and your lady will love you for it.

Ladies, I know how much you love it when a man takes charge and plans the date. It's sexy when a man behaves like a man. But what if he's a modern metrosexual who wants to get your input on where your date should be? If he asks your opinion, then it's your turn to get creative. Suggest a picnic in the park or a trip to the zoo. Or suggest something else that's fun in a retro sort of way. Roller skating? Bowling? Use your imagination!

Show him you're not afraid to think outside the dating box. With any luck, you will inspire him to up his game.

Love Magnet Rule #71

Sending a reply to a "break-up" email is a waste of time. Don't do it. Have a little self-respect. It's OK to write a reply if it makes you feel better. BUT DO NOT SEND IT.

After an enjoyable second date with a woman I really liked, I received a "Dear Chad" breakup email from her. I was quite disappointed, so I replied with an email of my own. I felt I needed to tell her she was making a mistake. She had not given our budding relationship the chance that it deserved.

That was a big mistake. There is no way to sound confident and desirable when your email says, "Wait! Don't go! I really like you! We could be great together! Please, don't go!"

Of course, that's not what I said in my email. But I might as well have, because that was the basic message. It was also the way I felt.

There was no way I was going to change her mind. Two seconds after I hit "send," I regretted it. Crap. What was I thinking? I knew better than that.

The next time I was dumped via email, I resisted sending an email in response. Oh, I *wrote* one. I called the woman a clueless witch who didn't have the sense to recognize me as one of the finest men who ever walked on planet Earth. I just had the good sense not to send it.

So, by all means, write the email after you've been dumped. Get the frustration out of your system. Be angry. Let off steam. You'll feel better for it.

But then hit the delete button.

Love Magnet Rule #72

Seek simplicity in a potential lover. If you find out that a man or woman has a complicated past or an unusual lifestyle, consider moving on. Otherwise, their baggage is going to become your baggage.

Love and relationships are difficult enough without adding unnecessary layers of complications and complexity. Some potential loves have more emotional and life baggage than others, so it's important to find out as soon as possible how much baggage they are bringing into their next relationship. Here are the Top Five Types of Relationship Baggage that you need to watch out for.

Top Five Types of Relationship Baggage

Kids. When you date someone with children, you are basically on a job interview to become the kids' stepparent. That's just the way it is, and you have to be comfortable with that if you're going to pursue the relationship.

Ex-Spouses and Ex-Lovers. The fewer of these the better. You probably don't want to date someone who still has a really close relationship with their ex—like still celebrating Thanksgivings and Christmases together. Can you spell C-O-M-P-L-I-C-A-T-E-D?

Parents and Other Family Members. If there are other family members living with the person, then you have to remember that you'll soon be dealing with them too. For example, dating a single dad who also lives with his mother introduces all kinds of complications. Sure, he has a built-in babysitter for his kids. But one day in the future, there's probably going to be a date that includes them all—your new love, his kids, his mother, and you. Are you sure you can handle that?

Craziness. Sometimes this is hard to pick up on during an early date. But whenever a potential new love begins to reveal some underlying crazy beliefs or behavior, get the hell out. If they whip out tarot cards and wads of Bigfoot hair, and then want to do a "reading" on you, it's probably time to leave.

Financial Troubles. If you're a financially responsible person and you're dating a financial flake, you're heading toward trouble. Fast forward a couple of years to the two of you as a married couple. He's spending all your money and your credit score has taken a dive. I'm just sayin'.

If you are simply looking for a good time, the complexities of additional baggage won't be as big a deal to you. But if you're truly a Love Magnet who is looking for "happily ever after," then keep your eyes open to possible red flags. Don't forget your "deal breakers"—the things that you won't tolerate in a relationship.

Love Magnet Rule #73

Don't let the odds get you down.
Just because every couple you know is breaking up
doesn't mean that you can't meet someone, fall in love,
and live happily ever after.

One of the most-often cited statistics is this: one out of every two modern marriages ends in divorce. It turns out that calculating the actual divorce rate is more complex than simply dividing the number of marriages in any given year by the number of divorces during that same year. Some sources say the actual divorce rate is closer to 33 percent. But whatever the figure really is, no one will argue that *a lot* of marriages end up in divorce.

If you were to calculate the percentage of romantic couples that break up *before* they got married, that number would be shockingly high. Do you really want to venture into love and commitment—and possibly marriage—if the path is so fraught with failure?

That's a question each one of us has to answer. A true Love Magnet will answer, "Yes!" As Harrison Ford said while playing the Star Wars hero Han Solo, "Never tell me the odds." Like Mr.

Solo, a Love Magnet chooses to remain optimistic no matter what kind of evidence there is to the contrary.

Consider what your life will be like as a perpetually single adult, growing old alone. Compare that to your life as a happily married person or a person who is in a happy, committed relationship, sharing the best that life has to offer. It's a proven fact that those who are married are happier and live longer than single people.

The truth is, you can look around you and find evidence to support whatever you want to believe. You can focus on couples breaking up and getting divorced, or you can concentrate on the couples who are deeply in love and devoted to their partners.

If you choose the path of love, then know in your heart that love is out there in the form of a wonderful new love who is perfect for you. Believe that it is possible to fall in love again—no matter who you are, what your relationship history is, or how old you are.

Love Magnet Rule #74

Watch for body language clues that a potential love is starting to get interested in you. Smiles, prolonged direct eye contact, and less personal space between the two of you are signs of interest and sexual attraction.

Potential new loves will let you know when they are attracted to you. Sometimes they will boldly tell you. More commonly, though, potential loves will communicate their attraction with subtle clues. But most of us have so much chatter going on in our own heads that we don't pay attention to the clues.

Before most people give you verbal clues about their attraction to you, their bodies will start telling you. Entire books have been written about how body language reveals sexual attraction. (There's even a *Body Language for Dummies* book!) So, I'm not going to go into great detail here. But watch for these signs of attraction:

Prolonged eye contact. If he is looking you in the eyes for longer than a polite second or two, he's communicating his attraction. (Women do the same thing when they are attracted to a man.) This is the most reliable early sign of attraction.

Open body versus closed body. Crossed arms and tightly crossed legs are a bad sign in the dating world. Try to pay attention to the moment he goes from crossed arms and legs to a more open body position. That's when you're starting to get his interest. Men will also adopt a stance or body posture that literally "takes up more space" in an effort to impress you.

The "personal space" zone gets smaller. When someone is willing to accept less physical distance between them and you, that's a sure sign of attraction. "Violating" personal space by gently touching someone's arm or body during a conversation is one way of showing interest. If he or she welcomes your friendly touches—and especially if the touches are returned, that's a demonstration of interest and physical attraction.

Women, in particular, will show interest and attraction with their conversation. (As you already know, women are *significantly* more verbal than men.) A woman will quickly ask a man about his job, his relationship status, and other basic things. As she gets to know him better and she delves deeper, she will try to get him to talk about his last relationship. She'll want to know how long the relationship lasted. How long ago was the breakup? Why did the relationship end?

She's evaluating him, determining if he is ready for a new relationship. She'll ask questions that will reveal how dependable he is, if he can be trusted, and if he is worthy of her heart. Often these fact-finding attempts are subtle. But how he responds will determine what kind of relationship she will have with him—none, temporary, or potentially long-term.

Men won't delve so deeply as quickly. A man's questions will be less penetrating, and he will infuse much of his fact finding with humor. "So, just how crazy was your ex-lover?" he might ask lightheartedly. He will be doing the male thing: trying to look cool while gathering information he can use.

But don't expect too much of him too soon. It shouldn't surprise you if he's still at the "she's got great boobs!" stage and you're already thinking, "I think he'd be a great dad!"

Love Magnet Rule #75

Sometimes Love Magnets clean toilets.
Especially if it will impress a potential lover.

Here's a gross generalization for you: the average woman does more housework than the average man. The average woman also does a *better job* of housework than the average man. I don't care how much housework men say they do, most studies show that even a "modern" man who cohabitates with a woman doesn't do his fair share of the housework.

Nevertheless, neither men nor women want to get involved in a relationship with a total slob. It's not a turn-on at all.

At some point during your dating, you will invite a new love to your place. You will be judged on how clean your apartment or house is. You will be *severely* judged on how clean your toilet is.

This is true for both women and men. Since the typical man's apartment isn't likely to be as clean as the typical woman's apartment, men are at a disadvantage in this department. Men, if you haven't cleaned your toilet and you invite a woman back to your place, it could be the beginning of the end. And the empty pizza boxes and beer bottles aren't going to score you any points either.

So clean up your act.

Ladies, it might not be fair, but the standards are even higher for you. If your place is a mess when your new man arrives, you are going to lose a lot of relationship points. So clean up your apartment—and your toilet—or he's going to think you are a slob.

He doesn't want you to be a slob. Deep down, he knows he's a slob—and the thought of two slobs potentially living together is depressing to him. God knows, he can be a slob without your help.

So, whether you're a woman or a man—clean up your place before your date arrives.

Love Magnet Rule #76

First, date your prospective love.
Then introduce him to your kids.

One of the most common questions among divorced singles is, "When should I let my date meet my children?" I always say, "At least 30 minutes before the wedding."

Just kidding. An hour before the wedding would be better.

Ha! I'm still kidding. The real answer is there's not a single right answer. But one of the fastest ways to scare a potential love away is to introduce your kids into the dating process too soon.

A first date should involve two people. That's also true for second and third dates. And probably fourth and fifth dates too. Early dates are for grownups to get to know each other.

If you bring your kids into the picture too soon, it looks like you're more interested in finding a stepparent for your kids than a lover for yourself.

I experienced the truth of this rule firsthand. In fact, one of the worst dates I ever went out on was with the most beautiful woman I ever dated. After a delightful (but slightly strange) first date, the woman I now call the Yoga Goddess invited me to her house for dinner. Actually, she invited me for dinner with her and her daughter.

I rang the doorbell at her house and the smell of incense wafted out the door as the Yoga Goddess greeted me. She was wearing a slinky, long dress that hugged her hips and her breasts. She was stunningly beautiful, and I thought how lucky I was to be spending time with her.

I got a grand tour of the house, of course, and I met the daughter of the Yoga Goddess. Unfortunately, the daughter did not strike me as particularly bright, friendly, or talented.

During the next two hours, I heard a lot of, "Mom! Look at this!" as the daughter tried desperately to get her mother's attention. It was annoying—and exhausting.

From the Yoga Goddess, I heard about how special her daughter was. I heard about how much she would benefit from a strong father figure in her life. I began to get more and more uncomfortable with the way the evening was unfolding.

This was not the way I wanted the date to go. I was supposed to be getting to know the Yoga Goddess. I was supposed to be gazing into her eyes and gazing into her soul. And a little kissing would have been nice too.

Alas, it was not to be. The Yoga Goddess did not realize that the man and the woman must date first. Once a bond has begun between them, then and only then can kids be added to the mix.

I never saw the Yoga Goddess again.

Love Magnet Rule #77

A relationship with a partner with children will ultimately include the kids. So if you hate his or her kids (or they hate you), the odds are the romantic relationship isn't going to be permanent.

This Love Magnet Rule is a natural extension of the previous rule. Unfortunately, after you've met the other person's kids, they can become deal breakers in the new relationship. Sometimes the kids won't like you, or you won't like the kids—or both.

I once had a serious relationship with a woman whose daughter, Becky, hated me. Well, she might not have exactly hated me, but she acted like I was a big jerk, and she basically ignored me. The feeling was mutual, because I thought Becky had the personality of a goldfish. When our paths crossed, Becky would swim out of the room without acknowledging my presence.

I tried to be nice to Becky. I was friendly. I cut her a lot of slack. But no matter how hard I tried, I got zero from Becky. I think Becky was simply tired of having to meet a procession of men who her mother brought home over the years, so she took it out on me.

Looking back on it now, Becky was a big reason that I broke up with her mom. I did not want to have to deal with Becky for the rest of my life.

Sometimes you get lucky and you love your boyfriend's kids—and they grow to love you. That's great when that happens. In other cases, kids can be tough on Mom's or Dad's new romantic friend. But kids can also be welcoming and forgiving when they are given a chance to get to know a new mother or father figure. Treat them with love, kindness, and respect, and even reluctant kids will tend to warm up to you.

So I'm not saying that bringing kids into a new relationship is a *bad* thing. I'm just saying that it's a *big* thing, and you're going to have to work it out.

Love Magnet Rule #78

If you and your new love are going to have sex, your kids are going to find out about it. Assuming they are old enough to understand what is happening, it is far better to talk to them about it up front than for them to discover it embarrassingly on their own.

One of the reasons modern adult dating can be confusing is that the so-called experts disagree on many aspects of dating. The "expert" advice on the topic of the dating sleepover is as varied and plentiful as Hollywood divorces.

The advice ranges from the heartfelt (just be honest and straightforward in a way that is age appropriate for your children) to the practical (soundproof your bedroom with extra pillows under the door and behind your headboard).

The real key to dealing with something this important—and inevitable—is to know your kids. The proper way to deal with sleepovers has a lot to do with your parenting style, the age and emotional maturity of your kids, and how open and honest you are with your kids.

After her divorce, Diana was able to avoid dealing with this topic for quite a while because her daughter was away at school.

But when her daughter came back for the summer, Diana had to talk to her about sex—Diana's sex life, not her daughter's. She broached the subject as nonchalantly as possible. One evening, Diana told her daughter that she was going out with her boyfriend to a movie, and afterward she would be returning home with him. The boyfriend might spend the night. And he wouldn't be sleeping in the guest room.

"Are you going to have a problem with that?" Diana asked.

Her daughter looked at Diana like she was a ridiculous, old-fashioned fool.

"No, why would it be a problem?"

"Well, we're going into new territory here, and I didn't want to upset you or embarrass you," said Diana.

Again, Diana got the "ridiculous old fool" look.

"I've just spent a whole year living away from home at college, so I know that women and men spend the night with each other sometimes. I'm nearly 20. I can handle it."

And that was it.

You might not get off as easily as Diana did. It depends on the ages of your kids, what they think of your new love, how protective they are of you, and dozens of other factors.

But you'll figure it out. It's what parents do.

Love Magnet Rule #79

A vacation getaway can be a fabulous way to get to know your lover—for better or for worse. Spending days together without a break will let you see "the real" person.

Vacations are fun. Vacations are exciting. Vacation sex is exciting. Going on a vacation with your new lover so that you can have vacation sex is especially exciting. Frankly, I'm surprised that anyone is willing to go back home when they can stay on vacation and keep having vacation sex.

Of course, there's more to vacations than vacation sex. A vacation getaway with your romantic partner is a great way to get to know him or her better. The first time you venture out on a vacation with your lover will probably be the most intensive, longest amount of nonstop time you've ever spent alone together.

My friend, Sarah, once told me she uses her Boyfriend Vacations as opportunities to move her relationships to the next level. If she is interested in a man and they have been dating for a while, she suggests to him that they go on an out-of-town trip to a place that sounds fun and exotic. Then she does everything she can to bond with him in a deeper and more meaningful way.

Spending every moment together for several days is a crash course in getting to know someone. After a few days, your defenses break down. Through familiarity or simple exhaustion, you begin to show elements of your true personality that you can keep completely hidden during three-hour dates. Sarah said a vacation trip can bond her with a new love in ways that would take months of normal dating.

But Sarah's approach has also backfired. She once made the mistake of going on a trip to the south of France for three weeks with a man she had known for only a few months. Before they left, there were signs that maybe their relationship wasn't built to last. But she ignored the signs because she wanted to go drink French wine, eat French cheese and bread, and have French sex with her American boyfriend. The first five days of their vacation were great, and the next five days were fine but not spectacular. But on day 11 her new love had a meltdown. Sarah saw all his faults and flaws—all at once.

The good news: Sarah broke up with him after they got back home because it was clear he wasn't The One.

The bad news: The last part of her vacation in France with her soon-to-be ex-boyfriend was tense, tense, tense.

You might want to start with a long weekend trip, so your new love won't drive you literally crazy—and vice versa.

Love Magnet Rule #80

Breakups don't have to be angry,
confrontational, or hurtful.

Men can be clueless, heartless bastards. As a man, I know this to be true, and sometimes I am ashamed of male behavior. Men not only behave like self-centered clueless bastards, but at times men even seem to enjoy breaking women's hearts.

But in defense of the masculine gender, I must say that most good plumbers, chefs, quarterbacks, politicians, and brain surgeons are men. If you want to unclog a stopped-up toilet or need to hit a wide receiver 25 yards downfield, call a man.

If you want to learn a lesson of the heart, however, your best bet is to call a woman.

I learned the truth of this Love Magnet Rule from a girlfriend with whom I was about to break up. We both knew the breakup was coming. In fact, we even scheduled a breakup meeting. "We need to talk—in person," I told her on the phone.

I was all geared up for an emotional confrontation—complete with plenty of accusations and blame. The only breakups in my life had involved sadness, anger, and arguments. By the time my soon-to-be-ex-girlfriend knocked on my door, I had a detailed list in my head of just how bad and wrong she was.

Then my girlfriend gave me a wonderful gift. She arrived with a smile on her face. We both knew this was a breakup, but the wiser participant in this meeting (my girlfriend) knew that it didn't have to be ugly and angry.

We sat on my couch and talked. She apologized to me for her faults and her failures. That inspired me to do the same. We ended up saying how much we cared about each other. Then we mutually decided that our relationship could go no further, so it was time for both of us to move on.

This woman showed me that a "breakup" doesn't have to be angry or hurtful. Nobody has to be the bad guy, and no one has to be wrong. Sometimes two people who are not destined to be together can simply agree to venture forward on their own separate paths.

Whether you are a woman or a man, if you are actively dating and still looking for your perfect love partner you're probably going to experience a breakup or two. When that happens, try to be as enlightened and kind as you can. Take the lead in being grateful for the time the two of you spent together. At the same time, be clear that it's time to move on.

A breakup doesn't have to involve yelling, blaming, and name-calling. It's not about you being right and the other person being wrong. It's about respectfully ending a relationship so you're free to keep looking for the love of your life.

Love Magnet Rule #81

Make sure a potential love knows your name.
Repeat your name just to make sure.

This is great advice for any Love Magnet in a dating situation—and whenever you're in a non-dating social setting too.

You've been in the situation where you meet someone for the first time, you hear their name, you shake their hand, and then you immediately forget their name—right? We all have.

Well, you will make friends and be the hit of the Yacht Club (or wherever you are at the time) if you always reintroduce yourself the next time you meet someone, repeating your name to make sure they remember it.

This is an especially good technique on the singles circuit. Whenever you meet a member of the opposite sex for the second and sometimes even third time, always smile and repeat your name. If the other person has that look in their eyes that says, "Oh shit, what was her name again?" then you will see the relief in his eyes when you reintroduce yourself.

If, on the other hand, a man says, "Oh sure, I remember you," then you can follow up with a seductive smile and a comment like,

"I just wanted to make *absolutely* sure you remembered my name." All the while, you smile seductively as you gaze into his eyes.

Yes, it sounds corny. But try it out. This technique really works. You'd be surprised how many singles are not brave enough to let their interest in someone be known early on. Letting them know that you're interested—especially in a safe, socially acceptable way—is a great way to stand apart from all the other chicken-hearted singles. Plus, being just a touch "forward" can be quite attractive. It means you know what you want and you are not afraid to go for it.

A great love affair can start with a warm handshake—and making sure the person who interests you knows your name.

Love Magnet Rule #82

The more handsome or beautiful someone is, the more often they have been told of their physical attractiveness. To stand out from other prospective suitors, start with a compliment that has nothing to do with how great they look.

Have you ever watched *The Bachelor* show on TV? (It's OK to admit it. There are millions of us in the "Bachelor Nation" who secretly watch the show.) If you have watched the first show of any season of *The Bachelor,* you've seen the procession of gorgeous women getting out of limousines to meet the new bachelor. And what does he say to each woman? "You look beautiful" or "Hi, you're gorgeous."

The same thing happens when it's *The Bachelorette.* The parade of handsome men who arrive to meet Miss Bachelorette are told how great they look in their suits and tuxedoes.

Of course, in every case it's true. The women and men are all gorgeous. They've been cast for a TV show, and how they look is important to the ratings. But this is a group of singles who have been told time and time again how physically attractive they are.

They are used to it, and it almost doesn't mean anything to them anymore.

In the real world, starting with a "you look great!" compliment is precisely the wrong way to approach a beautiful woman or a handsome man. Think about how many times a really gorgeous woman has been told by men (some of them quite creepy) that she's beautiful or sexually desirable. And how many times have women fawned over an attractive man? As wonderful as it is to be told that you're physically attractive, don't you think that would get a little tiresome? Attractive men and beautiful women also want to be appreciated for their minds, for their accomplishments, and for the dozens of other reasons that make them individual and special.

That's why, if you want to stand apart from everyone else, you shouldn't start with a compliment about their good looks. And men, don't approach a beautiful woman with a lewd remark about how hot she is and how much you'd like to get her into bed. That *is not* going to get you her approval and affection.

Don't be like other men who tell her she looks like a swimsuit model or an angel. Don't be like other women who get star-struck by a man's physical attractiveness and can't think of anything else to talk about. Instead, ask a question about a current event that's been in the news. Make a witty comment about the restaurant you're in. Or mention that they're giving off a spiritual vibe. Get the conversation going in a completely different direction.

After you get to know him or her, you'll have plenty of opportunities to tell him he's a Greek god or she's gorgeous enough to be in movies.

You're So Hot . . .

If you *insist* on leading with a comment about physical attractiveness, there's only one way to make it work. You have to be playful about it. You have to be so over the top that he or she gets that you're giving a compliment—while at the same time you're being ironically funny.

Here are some entertaining opening lines that focus on physical beauty. But please heed this warning: these lines only work if you deliver them confidently and with a smile. You have to be all-in with your delivery for these to work.

- You are so hot, when I look at you I get a tan.
- You must be in the wrong place. The Miss Universe contest is at the Hilton.
- You look like an angel. What are you doing here on Earth?
- Is it hot in here or is it just you?
- If beauty were time, you would be an eternity.
- Did you get your license suspended for driving all these girls crazy?
- What's a nice girl/guy like you doing with a body like that?
- Can you kiss me on the cheek so I can say a handsome man kissed me tonight?"

On second thought, forget these pickup lines and say something more intelligent. The love of your life probably wants to have a *real* conversation with you.

Love Magnet Rule #83

If you discover that you have been doing something that your dates or your potential dates don't like, stop doing it. You can't be a Love Magnet if you are chasing the loves away.

After her divorce, Amanda took some time to get her life back together. She knew she wasn't ready to get into dating right away. Instead, she joined a book club and met some new friends. She also took a class at a local community college to get in touch with her inner artist.

When she felt she was ready for dating again, she stuck her toe in the dating waters by giving online dating a try. She chose a screen name and began writing her profile by responding to the prompts on the website. Her friend took a photo of her and uploaded it to the site.

Feeling empowered, she then waited for the responses from eligible single men. And she waited. Then she waited some more.

What had she done wrong? A male friend took one look at her profile and knew what her first mistake was. "I think you need a new photo," he suggested. (Her photo made her look frumpy.) He also suggested that her profile text be rewritten to highlight the fun things she liked to do and her new hobbies.

These changes made all the difference. Amanda's dating calendar began to fill up.

I have a similar story. When I first tried online dating, I thought that meeting women online was going to be easy. I thought I would simply have to send out some well-written emails and I would have women lining up for the chance to go out on a date with me. How hard could it be?

I sent emails to 26 women I found online, but I received just four responses. When I responded to these four lovely women, I received two follow-up emails. Of these two, I set up a Meet and Greet date with one woman.

That was a pathetic success rate. What was I doing wrong?

Well, according to a female friend who was more familiar with online dating than I was, the emails I was sending were *way too long*.

"I don't even respond to the long messages," my friend said. "It's too much like work. But if someone sends me a nice, short message, I try to respond with a nice, short reply."

All this time I thought my patented, well-crafted, highly detailed and *long* emails were love magnets, but instead they were *love repellents*. Women weren't responding to me because it was too much work.

That was a humbling thing to learn, and as a result I quickly changed my approach. Instead of lengthy messages that told my life story, I started sending one-line comments and questions such as, "Hey, where was that photo taken?" or "Where is the most romantic beach you've ever been to?"

The results were immediate. The next day, I had 15 supermodels asking me for dates. Suddenly, I was the most popular single man in town.

All right, the results weren't *that* amazing. But the response rate soared, and I finally felt like I had gotten the hang of online dating.

I had learned a valuable lesson about dating and relationships. Whenever you discover you're doing something that isn't working, try doing something else. This goes for everything from your online dating behavior and what you wear on a first date to what you talk about during your dates and your attitude about the entire dating process.

If you are paying attention, it's never too late to learn something new.

Do you have a dating or relationship story? Check out Chad Stone's blog at www.chadstone.us.

Love Magnet Rule #84

Never appear desperate. No one is attracted to a person who is desperate for a date or desperate for a relationship.

Desperate is not attractive. Pathetic is not sexy. Needy is not what men are looking for. A whiny tone of voice is not what makes men want to get close.

One of the keys to becoming a Love Magnet is to act like you don't really care whether you find love. Because, ironically, appearing to not care about whether you find love (and the confidence that goes with it) is a great way to attract love.

True Love Magnets are already happy, whole, and complete— so they don't get their egos deflated if men or women don't notice them—or even if they are occasionally rejected.

When you think and act like a Love Magnet, it doesn't make any difference whether one particular person is attracted to you or talks to you. You know why? Because there's always another potential love to talk to in the next restaurant, walking along the next street, or sitting *right over there*. Why get upset and frustrated when your next true love might be just minutes away?

Women, especially smart, single women, can smell desperation. It smells like a cross between a wet dog and a stale beer, and the smell of desperation turns them off completely. When a woman smells the odor of desperation on a man, she will often run toward the nearest "Bad Boy" type. A Bad Boy never acts desperate or pathetic. He knows there are plenty of women out there.

Now the average Bad Boy is probably not looking for a soul mate. He's probably just looking to get laid. On the evolutionary scale of men, he's the closest thing to a caveman that you're going to see walking around in a modern urban jungle. He's not looking for Miss Right, he's looking for Miss Ready-for-Sex-Right-Now.

Most men have behaved like an unevolved Bad Boy now and then. They might have even gotten laid because of their Bad Boy persona. But when they lose their Bad Boy mojo, they start feeling sorry for themselves—and they couldn't attract a woman if they walked into a packed show of the Las Vegas male revue, Thunder From Down Under.

Women have experienced the female version of this when they have gotten frustrated with men and adopted an "I don't care if I meet another man because I am happy with myself" attitude. That's usually when the men start coming over to hit on them. But when women go from "I don't care" to "I will never find a man, oh woe is me," then men disappear like free beers at a frat party.

Whenever you lose your self-confidence and your dating mojo, your mantra should be: "I am a Love Magnet, and I will meet my perfect love at the perfect time."

When you act like you believe that, love will find you.

Love Magnet Rule #85

If you're going to be a Love Magnet, you need to keep learning about the opposite sex.

If you're a woman, and your goal is to become a Love Magnet so you can attract one special man into your life, you will need to continually learn about men. If you're a man, I absolutely guarantee that you will never become a Love Magnet unless you consciously keep trying to understand women. There's always more to learn about the opposite sex. There's always something new you can add to your repertoire to attract, impress, and delight potential new loves.

Let's start with the men. You know why men can't figure out women? It's because women are complicated creatures. There are at least 14 different thoughts operating in a woman's mind at all times. Men, on the other hand, are simple creatures. The typical man can only think one thought or do one thing at a time. His brain is usually consumed with a single thought of food, sex, sports, sex, internal combustion engines, sex, how great the woman over there looks, work, beer, sex, or sex.

Men and women can't figure each other out because they are fundamentally different. A man's brain is hardwired to go from

Point A to Point B in a logical, linear fashion. Detours and distractions confuse a man's brain. Using emotions to solve problems *really* confuses men. Men often don't know how to relate to women because, to them, a woman's brain is a jumble of unrelated thoughts and emotions.

Women can't figure out men because they can't believe men are so *simple*. Women make the mistake of believing that men think just like women. Wrong, wrong, wrong! Women don't realize that men do most of their problem solving internally, inside their own heads. They don't want to talk about it. They don't want to examine every idea verbally, saying it out loud to see how it sounds—the way women do.

Consequently, men and women make all kinds of mistakes during the dating ritual without even knowing it. And even worse, both men and women start believing they know all about the other gender. Women believe they know what men are like, and men think they know women.

Wrong, wrong, and wrong.

So, from that challenging foundation, each of us attempts to build a relationship with a member of the opposite sex. And now you know why I included "keep learning about the opposite sex" as a Love Magnet Rule.

You can spend years studying human behavior and the differences between men and women. I suggest that you keep your eyes, ears, and mind open so you can continue to learn. Here are some observations about men and women to get you in the mood for learning:

A man will melt when a woman appreciates his company.

A woman will grow fond of a man who actually listens to what she says. True listening involves not just hearing the words, but also adding the little nods and verbal responses that shows he is *actively* listening.

A man loves it when a woman knows how to cook. He also loves it when a woman is willing to cook *with him.*

A woman never gets tired of receiving flowers.

A man doesn't like it when you talk about your problems. It bums him out.

A woman doesn't like it when you don't share your day with her—even some of the problems and frustrations.

A man likes a woman who has a touch of spontaneity.

A woman will let you know by her behavior and her words when she likes what a man does. A man needs to pay attention, so he can do more of what she likes.

A man wants his woman to be happy. When she is happy, he is happy.

A woman is attracted to a man's strength—both mental and physical. That strength tells her that he will protect her.

A woman wants to be loved.

A man wants to be appreciated and respected.

A man values loyalty.

A woman values loyalty even more.

Whether you're a woman or a man, the key to winning—and keeping—the heart of your one true love is to keep learning what your lover likes and keep doing more of it. This isn't always easy. In fact, sometimes it's difficult, demanding, and exhausting. But if you've found the right partner, it's totally worth it.

So embrace the challenge. Relish the knowledge that you will never fully understand the opposite sex. There is always more you can learn—and that's one of the reasons love is so appealing.

Love Magnet Rule #86

Bring the very best of you to every date and to every relationship.

You are an incredible human being. You are capable of amazing acts of love and kindness. You have infectious energy and a desire to make your world a better place. You've probably given money to the homeless or stopped to help a stranger in need. You have given hugs and words of encouragement to friends and loved ones. You might have literally given the shirt off your back to someone or saved an animal in a shelter by bringing it home.

You are also sexy and desirable. You bring a long list of wonderful qualities to a relationship, and one special person will be lucky to be your partner. Your tenderness, humor, compassion, spirit of adventure, capacity for love, and willingness to commit to love make you an incredible life partner. And these are just *some* of the wonderful things you bring to a relationship.

The best version of you is the person to bring to every date. Leave your baggage behind. Do not bring the version of you who is full of self-doubts and "I'm not good enough" thoughts.

When you bring the best version of you to a date or to a relationship, you will encourage the other person to rise to your level. The best of you will bring out the best in them.

If they can't rise to your level, it will be painfully obvious. If they can't rise to your higher vibrational level, you will see it clearly—and quickly. This clarity will save you a lot of time and energy. This clarity is your friend.

The best of you will know whether your date has the potential to be your relationship partner. If there is no potential, you can quickly and easily move on. But if you feel the potential, because the best of you is relating to the best in them, then you will open yourself to the promise of a new relationship.

Love Magnet Rule #87

There is no way to force the chemistry of attraction—
no matter how hard you try.

Have you ever been on a blind date? Have you even been set up for a date with a friend of a friend, and arrived not knowing much about that person except "you're perfect for each other!"? But you went, hoping that when you met, lightning would strike.

We don't hear as much about blind dates as we used to. In a way, online dating is the 21st-century version of the blind date. However, before most online first dates, you typically see photos of each other. You've probably emailed each other too. If you're lucky, you've even talked to each other on the phone. You're not going in totally blind.

But whether you're arriving for an actual blind date or the modern equivalent, you're still hoping for one thing. You're hoping to meet someone and experience that wonderful sensation called chemistry. Because no matter how well you've been prepped with emails or phone calls, the chemistry of attraction only happens one way. It happens in person.

"Chemistry" between two people is one of those things that can't be forced. It's wonderful and exhilarating—and it's totally beyond your control.

It's mysterious and hard to explain, but if you're paying attention, your heart will tell you if there's any chemistry between you and your date. Most men say they usually know within two minutes of meeting a woman if there was any chemistry. Some can sense it right away. For others, it takes longer.

When I first met Krista, the lovely woman who is now my wife, I felt the chemistry almost instantly. Our Meet and Greet date was one chemical spark after another. Our first date lasted more than three hours over two locations, and it was—by far—the best first date in the history of the universe. Well, for me it was.

I have since learned that women experience chemistry differently than men do. For women, attraction is a more complicated experience. Women have more patience than men in most things, and that includes waiting to see if they feel an attraction toward someone new. So a man might feel the initial rush of "chemistry" in two minutes, while a woman might need a couple of hours—or longer—to feel that same rush of attraction.

But don't get too upset if you feel the chemistry right away and your date doesn't. Give him or her a chance to catch up. But if the chemistry isn't mutual, and that's really important to you, you're going to have to keep looking. The chemistry of love can't be forced—no matter how hard you try.

As I write this, I am sitting at a coffee shop. At the next table are a man and a woman who are obviously having a Meet and Greet date. They are both reasonably attractive, and they are both trying to be friendly. But there is no chemistry between them. I can tell by the way he's *not* gazing into her eyes that he's never going to call her again.

Like I said, there's no way to force chemistry. It either happens or it doesn't.

Love Magnet Rule #88

Be a lady. Be a gentleman. There are so few ladies and gentlemen left in the world these days, and being one is a great way to set yourself apart from all of the jerks in the dating world.

The world doesn't need any more assholes. There are enough male jerks and narcissists in the world. There are enough catty bitches in the world too. Take a vow right now to be a lady or a gentleman. Treat people with the respect that they deserve. Treat everyone with common courtesy (which, sadly, isn't as common as it used to be).

Advice for Women

When a man opens a door for you, graciously smile and thank him as you walk through.

Don't dominate the conversation. Yes, you will probably talk more than he does, but it's not a real conversation unless he contributes.

Ask questions about him and listen to the answers.

Don't swear.

Tell the truth.

Put your damn cell phone away.

Talk about the positive things that are happening in your life. Don't dwell on the negative things.

Don't trash talk about anyone.

If he calls you, pick up the phone. If he texts you, answer him.

If you need to reject him because you're not feeling the attraction or the chemistry, do it gently but firmly.

When he takes you out and pays the bill, express your appreciation.

Dress one step nicer than everyone else.

Allow him to be a man. Don't try to turn him into a woman.

Expect him to be a gentleman. If he's not, teach him to become one. If he can't be educated, move on to someone who can be.

When he gives you a compliment, smile and say "Thank you."

Always look for the best in other people.

Advice for Men

When you tell a woman that you're going to call her, then call her.

Hold the door open for her.

Walk over to the passenger side of the car and open the door for her. Then close it when she's safely inside.

Pull the chair out for her when you're getting seated in a restaurant.

Ask for her opinion and listen to the answer.

When you've had a wonderful time with her, thank her.

If you haven't had a wonderful time with her and you don't want to see her again, gently tell her that too. Don't make her wonder if she'll hear from you during the next week or two. That's torture.

Put your damn cell phone away.

When she talks to you, listen.

Tell the truth.

If she's cold, let her wear your jacket.

Never break up with her via text.

Treat her with respect, and treat her as you would like to be treated.

Always look for the best in other people.

If you follow these tips, plus the many other related guidelines that follow in the spirit of being a lady or a gentleman, you help make the world a better place.

You will also win the heart of your love.

Love Magnet Rule #89

When you've said something stupid or
done something stupid, apologize.
Don't wait, because that just makes it worse.

Nobody is perfect. We all do and say stupid things.

When you are just getting to know someone, these mistakes can sometimes be magnified. You think to yourself, "If he's like that now, what is he going to be like when he's not on his best behavior?"

Or maybe it's you that has done or said something stupid, and you wish you could back up time so you could undo it.

When you've said something stupid, apologize. When you've behaved in a stupid, clueless, or selfish way, apologize. Admit your mistake. Own it. Apologize for it. Say you'll never do it again, and mean it.

Obviously, it's a good idea to *not* behave like a jerk. This is true in all areas of your life, not just in the dating and relationships part of your life. Strive to be self-aware enough to know when you've behaved like a jerk. Know when you have said or done something that has offended another person—even unintentionally. Whenever you behave like a jerk or offend someone, show your true character with a heartfelt apology.

If someone apologizes to you, accept it graciously. If you can tell his apology is honest and heartfelt, then forgive him. Unless, of course, he's always doing and saying stupid things, and his string of apologies is longer than a freight train. In that case, it's a character issue or he's just stupid. And you can't fix stupid.

Love Magnet Rule #90

Don't be afraid to be spontaneous—
especially if it will make your lover happy.

Even the best-laid plans of a modern Love Magnet can benefit from a little spontaneity. When the details of your well-laid plan start to fray around the edges, or completely fall apart, you've got to be willing to adapt.

Once, when a wonderful daytime date was about to end, my date clearly didn't want to say goodbye. My date plan had worked out perfectly, but I hadn't planned for an extended date.

It was still light outside as we strolled through the city streets. I was having a wonderful time, and so was my lady.

"What do you want to do now?" I asked.

She smiled. She knew that meant we didn't have to say goodbye right away. And yet, she wasn't quite sure she should make a suggestion. The date thus far had gone according to my plan. Would I be offended if she sent our date in another direction?

She suggested going to a place where we could listen to a live band. This was definitely not part of my plan, but I welcomed the suggestion. It sounded great, and she would not have suggested it unless she thought it was a good idea. So I said yes, and a terrific date kept going.

An unplanned diversion brought us closer together. The date continued well into the night, and I learned a valuable lesson about being flexible and spontaneous.

Love Magnet Rule #91

When you find something that makes your lover happy, keep doing it.

Men are hard-wired with a deep desire to find a woman and make that woman happy. Sure, men can be macho and seem aloof. Men can be difficult to communicate with, because most men are creatures of few words. But despite all that, there is something about the DNA coding of a man that makes him want to please his woman.

Women also like to please their men. But first, they want to see if a man is worth the effort of pleasing. In other words, a woman wants to be romanced. She wants a man to show he's willing to do what it takes to win her love and affection. Once he has proven himself to her, she is more than happy to work hard to please him.

So as a relationship develops, both women and men can strengthen the growing bond of affection between them by paying attention to what makes their partner happy. Then do more of it.

Some Advice for Women

If he likes it when you wear a particular outfit, make sure you wear it for him.

If your man needs some time for his guy friends, give him the space and "permission" to have a night with the guys. You can use this time to see your girlfriends.

When you find out what he likes in bed, give it to him as long as you're comfortable with it.

Get to know his moods. If he needs to retreat to his "man cave," let him. Then gently coax him back with the promise of something delicious or passionate.

Tell him you love him, and tell him his strength makes you feel safe.

Encourage him. Sometimes men love having a cheerleader.

When he does something nice for you, thank him for it.

Remember to have fun. One of the things he liked about you in the beginning was your spirit of fun. Be fun—and encourage him to be fun too.

Some Advice for Men

If you learn that your love has a favorite restaurant, take her there more than once.

If you find out she likes flowers, keep bringing her flowers.

Keep your emotional heart open. She wants to be part of your life, and she loves it when you talk about your life with her.

If your woman loves getting her feet rubbed, learn how to give the best amateur foot massages.

If you discover that she loves it when you say, "I love you," then look into her beautiful eyes and say, "I love you."

If she likes it when you call her when you're leaving work, call her to let her know when you'll be home.

Don't take her for granted.

Hugs and kisses at unexpected times go a long way toward keeping her passion alive.

This isn't rocket science, and it's not difficult. You just need to pay attention to the cues your lover is giving you—and keep doing the things that he or she likes.

One more thing: it's OK to ask them what they like. Women, in particular, love it when their man asks what they like and what would make them happy. Just *asking* what they want makes them happy. Granted, a man won't be able to honor every request. She might be out of luck if she wants a $100,000 sports car or a diamond ring the size of a Christmas ornament.

Also, you also don't want to rearrange your *entire* life around pleasing your lover. Whether you're a woman or a man, there is a limit to what you can do—and what you are willing to do—to please your love partner. Men cannot give up their entire lives to please a woman without giving away some of their manhood, and most women who fall in love with a man want him to *continue to be* a man. A woman who demands too much can quickly turn into a "high maintenance" woman, who seems impossible to please. Men run from a woman like that.

So without being completely spineless, do what you can to keep your lover happy.

I always tell my lover that I'll protect her from foul balls when I take her to a baseball game. If she wants to go to a ballet, she's on her own.

Love Magnet Rule #92

Love Magnets know when to commit fully to the love of their dreams.

Some people believe dating is strictly a numbers game. You have to go out on a lot of dates in order to find the right lover for you. Some women call this "kissing a lot of frogs."

Dating might be a numbers game, but the only number that matters is *one*. Because the goal is to find the one person with whom you really want to spend your life.

When I met Krista, I knew that my search was over. I had found my love. It didn't matter that we lived in different cities more than an hour apart. It didn't matter that we each had houses and kids, and that our lives were destined to dramatically change if we kept seeing each other. I was ready to make a commitment. My dating days were over.

Not only was I enraptured by a delightful new romance, but my heart knew that this romance could last forever if I committed myself to it.

So I did. I had the lover I wanted. And that's my wish for everyone who embarks on the journey. May you find the woman or the man of your dreams, may you commit your heart and life fully to that lucky person, and may you both live happily ever after.

Bonus Rules

Tips for Keeping the Love of
Your Dreams Happy

It took 92 Love Magnet Rules to get here.

You became a Love Magnet so you could get the one special lover you really wanted. You have succeeded in becoming the most desirable version of you, and in doing so you won the heart of a man or woman who was once out of your league. You now have the Love of Your Dreams.

So what do you do now? I'll tell you what you do—you do everything you can to keep your love relationship vibrant and growing. And if your lover is truly the Love of Your Dreams, you will express and demonstrate your love every day.

Keeping the love alive isn't easy. Fortunately much of what you've already learned while becoming a Love Magnet is also valuable in keeping you and your lover happy in your growing relationship.

The nine Love Magnet Rules that follow build on what you've already learned. Now your focus isn't on finding and meeting a lover who is worthy of your affections. Now your focus is on showing the lover you have that you are worthy of his or her continued love and affection.

You're still a Love Magnet. But now there's only one person who matters to you. Use the following Love Magnet Rules to show your lover that you want to stay in love forever.

Love Magnet Rule #93

Keep dating your lover. Continue to use the behaviors you learned as a Love Magnet to make your loved one feel special.

I once thought the skills I learned to become a Love Magnet were going to be useless once I had a girlfriend. After all, I would no longer need outstanding verbal skills to strike up a friendly conversation with a woman I had just met. I would no longer need to be charming and appealing, and my gentlemanly behaviors could be retired. Once I found my true love, my Love Magnet job was over.

But now I know better. In a relationship, many of your Love Magnet skills become more important than ever.

Even though you are now in a loving relationship, it's important to keep using your Love Magnet skills to keep the romance alive. For example, one of the key ways to keep the love fire burning is to make time for "date nights." During your date nights, use your best manners and conversational skills, and bring the excitement you felt when you were first getting to know your love partner.

Love Magnet Rule #53 is significant when you are trying to win someone's heart—but it's even more important when you are working to keep your love strong. "When you find someone special, treat them like someone special." The longer you're with someone, the easier it is to forget how special that person is to you. Keeping yourself in "dating mode" is one way to remember how lucky you are.

Remember the chemistry the two of you felt when you were just getting to know each other? Keep it alive by setting aside a date night at least once a month. Go to your favorite restaurant—just the two of you. Gaze into each other's eyes and talk about how exciting your first dates were. Talk about the fun things that you want to do together in the future. Promise each other that you will keep your relationship a priority, and you will continue to appreciate each other.

Not every date night with your lover has to be a big night on the town. There is something delightful about staying in. If you've got kids, send them to Grandma's house or to sleepovers at friends' houses. Have a romantic dinner at home. (See Love Magnet Rule #38.) A carefully prepared dinner at home—complete with candles and flowers on the table—will help to keep the passion burning.

In between your date nights, do little things to show that you're still in love. Send texts at random times to say "I hope you're having a great day" and "Thinking nice thoughts about you." Hide love notes where your sweetie will find them. Be generous with foot rubs. Smile.

Anyone with relationship experience knows that love alone brings no guarantees. So keep showing your lover how much you care about him or her.

Love Magnet Rule #94

Agree on a code phrase that you and your love use to communicate "this is important to me."

This is a tool that my lovely wife taught me. When we got beyond the "dating" stage and into the "engaged" part of our relationship, our goal was to continue to keep the lines of communication open. Being able to talk to each other—and hear what the other has to say—is one of the keys to a healthy and happy relationship.

Women are naturally better at relationship communication than men. Men tend to tune out and retreat to their man caves. Even when men are physically present, sometimes their brains get up and leave the room. Without even trying, most men master the art of pretending to listen but hearing nothing.

When my lover realized that sometimes I was a world-class non-listener, she came up with a phrase that was code for *this is important to me*:

"It would mean the world to me if . . ."

When she says those words, I stop whatever I am doing and I give her my complete attention. With those few words, she gives me the gift of telling me what's really important to her. Without saying so exactly, she is telling me that I need to heed these words for the sake of our relationship. Whatever follows that magic phrase is Important with a capital I.

If she tells me, "it would mean the world to me if . . ." I pay attention. My dear lover is about to make a request that means a lot to her. And because it's an important request, I need to take her request seriously.

This technique has worked well for us, because we follow these three rules:

My love does not use the code phrase lightly. She never says, "It would mean the world to me if you took out the trash" or "It would mean the world to me if you put the toilet seat down." In order for the code phrase to remain effective, you can't use it frivolously.

If it is at all possible, I honor her request.

The code words are a two-way form of communication. I get to use the code phrase when I have an important request too.

I believe that the use of this code phrase has helped reduce friction in our relationship by helping us communicate what we really want. So agree with your lover to use this code phrase or something similar to help the two of you keep the lines of meaningful communication open.

Love Magnet Rule #95

Use cute pet names for your loved one to demonstrate your affection. And don't be embarrassed if other people hear you.

I call this the "snookums" rule. As couples, we seem to naturally invent cutesy monikers for that special someone in our lives. Experts say the use of pet names, such as Sweetie, Cutie Pie, Honeybunch, and Coo-Coo Butt, creates a kind of a boundary around a relationship. It's a way to identify the relationship as exclusive, and no one else but the two of you can get in.

When people overhear your lovey-dovey conversation, they know you're committed to each other. The fact that you have cutesy pet names for each other means that you are in a Relationship. Let me tell you, Cupcake, if you're calling your boyfriend or girlfriend by a pet name, then you should have already pulled your profile from Match.com.

Are there actual benefits derived from using silly, personalized names for our lovers? Apparently, yes. One study published in the *Journal of Social and Personal Relationships* reported that the more a couple uses endearing pet names and made-up terms, the higher their relationship satisfaction tends to be.

But please, don't overdue the whole Snookums stuff in front of other people. Pet names are cute to the couple who use them, but pet names are so sugary sweet to any other human being within earshot that they cause instant diabetic shock and a gagging reflex. (Have you ever noticed how many pet names are variations on sweet things? We're talking about everything from Honey and Muffin to Sugar and Sweet Cheeks. It turns out that we humans must really love sweet foods, and that carries over into the sweet names we give our Cutie Patooties.)

By the way, if you don't already have a cute pet name for your honey, then check out Pet Name Generator at www.links2love.com/nicknames.htm.

Love Magnet Rule #96

Say "I love you" every day.

This Love Magnet Rule should be obvious. Your sweetie loves to hear the words "I love you."

There's an old story that might be true, or it might be one of those made-up things used to make a point. But once there was a man who married his school sweetheart when they were still young. They had a nice wedding and they exchanged traditional vows.

After many decades of marriage, one of their children asked her dad, "Why do you never tell Mom that you love her?"

"I told her on the day that I married her that I loved her, and that hasn't changed," he said. "When I feel differently, I'll tell her."

That's a sad story about a clueless guy who doesn't know anything about how to keep a romance alive and well. So don't be like that clueless jerk. Instead, do this:

Look your sweetie in the eyes and say, "I love you."

Send loving text messages often—even as often as every day.

Give frequent hugs.

Leave little love notes where they will be found during the day.

Talk to each other.

Be nice. Treat each other with kindness and respect.

Help each other with the daily chores.

Smile at each other.

Tell him that he's sexy and he turns you on.

Tell her that she's beautiful and she turns you on.

Kiss him or her every night before you go to sleep and every morning when you wake up (you can wait in the morning until after he's brushed his teeth).

No one on this planet has ever complained about hearing "I love you" too many times. But millions of us wish their lover would say "I love you" more often.

Love Magnet Rule #97

Learn how to be a better listener. Listening is a powerful way to say "I love you."

There's a saying that goes, "You have two ears and one mouth because you should listen twice as much as you talk." When it comes to keeping a relationship healthy, that's brilliant advice. Communication is one of the pillars of a relationship, and listening to your partner is a powerful way to say "I love you" without ever opening your mouth.

Here are some tips to help make you a better listener:

Take the time to hear what the other person is saying and try to understand the situation from his or her perspective.

Try to refrain from going from listening mode to "fix it" mode. Sometimes the other person needs to process the issues that are troubling them. They don't need an immediate solution to their problem, they simply need to be heard.

Don't personalize the other person's problem. It's not about you, it's about them.

Give the other person your undivided attention. This is not the time to check emails or Facebook posts on your phone.

Use active listening techniques, such as nodding and making verbal sounds ("uh-huh," "hmmm," etc.) to let the other person know you are fully present.

If what you're hearing sounds like some reassurance is called for, let the other person know that you sympathize with him or her.

If you don't understand something, gently ask questions to clarify. This will get you the additional information you need, and it also communicates that you are listening.

Try to remember what you've heard. Chances are this issue or this story will come up again, so remembering the gist of the conversation will be helpful to both of you.

Don't interrupt. Listen.

Don't minimize or condescend with comments such as "You're making such a big deal about this."

When you do respond, use encouraging words that show you care. A supportive comment is often the best way to show you are hearing the other person.

It's almost always a good idea to end a conversation with your arms held wide and this loving statement: "It sounds like you could use a big hug."

Love Magnet Rule #98
Make your lover feel sexy—desirable, loved, and sexy.

Once upon a time, only a few decades ago, women weren't encouraged to be sexy. Women were told not to enjoy sex. The women who did enjoy sex back then were trashy, wanton hussies who smoked, drank, and were on the path straight to hell.

"Good girls" didn't behave like that at all. Good girls had sex a few times in their lives to procreate, and then they locked their genitals away in a box and threw away the key.

Thank your lucky stars that you live in the modern Western world, where women are allowed to acknowledge and experience their own sexuality. But even today, there's *desirable sexy* and there's *trashy sexy*. Most women don't want to feel trashy sexy.

What's the difference between the two kinds of sexy? For most women, *desirable sexy* is feeling like a modern sexual woman within the confines of a committed relationship. It's feeling safe enough to show your vulnerability and express your physical desires. It is feeling loved enough to literally bare your body and your soul.

Trashy sexy is over-the-top, slutty-clothes-wearing, pole-dancing,   sleep-with-anyone-who-happens-to-be-around   sexy.

Some women might go through a trashy-sexy phase to see what it's like, or they might have a trashy-sexy encounter on a night when they drank too many mojitos, but it's not a behavior that they're proud of when they get to be grown-up adults. Trashy sexy isn't the kind of behavior that you expect from PTA moms.

Sure, lots of couples dabble in trashy sexy behavior once in a while. Sometimes a conservative woman will talk dirty to her boyfriend or husband in the confines of their bedroom if it turns him on. She does that as a gift.

But what she really wants is to feel desirable sexy. She wants to be loved, she wants to be wanted, and she wants to be desired. She wants her lover to show his uncontrollable manly passion, and she wants him to show it to her exclusively.

So if you are in a committed, loving relationship, don't be afraid to show your sexy side. Your man wants to see it. (Boy, oh boy, does he want to see it.)

Men don't usually have any trouble showing their sexy side. Hell, they *always* want to show their sexy side. A smart, loving woman will help her man get in touch with his passionate side. She will show him there's a whole lot more to sex than orgasms. In fact, the tenderness and touch of foreplay can be the best part of sex.

So get your sexy on with your partner. Find out what your lover likes—and show your lover how to please you too.

Love Magnet Rule #99

Show your lover physical affection.

Remember when your romance was brand new? You couldn't keep your hands off each other. It started with the simple physical touches that connected your bodies. You walked hand-in-hand as you strolled down the street. You put your arms around each other. You snuggled up close when you sat next to each other so that your bodies were touching.

One of my favorite things is seeing a cute old couple in their 80s who are still holding hands as they walk through the mall. Or they still sit right next to each other on a park bench, their butts touching as he has his arm around her. They still show the world through their physical affection that they are in love.

Women love good, old-fashioned, PG-rated physical affection. Men like it too, but for many men they only demonstrate physical affection when they think it's the first step toward having sex.

The physical affection I'm talking about is *not* about getting laid. It's about demonstrating a level of love, affection, and commitment that is difficult to communicate in words alone. When you do this, effortlessly and often, it melts your lover's heart.

Love Magnet Rule #100

Never, ever take your love for granted.

Just because he or she is your lover today doesn't mean your love will last forever. That's right—you could blow it, if you don't behave yourself.

Here are just a few ways you could screw up by taking your love for granted:

Ways that Women Screw Up

You try too hard to change him. Men *will* change—at least a little bit. But they have to be convinced that there's something in it for them, and they have to believe it's their idea.

You nag him.

You pounce on him the minute he gets home. A man needs some "re-entry" time before he can pay full attention to what you're saying.

You forget to act like a woman. You know, the way you acted when you were dating.

You won't let him behave like a man. One of the biggest mistakes women make is trying to de-masculinize their men. And that ruins the dynamic of the relationship.

You don't give him any space for guy friends.

You talk too much—whether he's in the mood for it or not. He's never going to want to talk about your relationship the way you do. He's never going to want to talk about *anything* as much as you do. That's why it's important for you to have female friends.

You forget to seduce him once in a while. Sure, you're tired. We're all tired. But that's still no excuse.

Ways that Men Screw Up

You turn into a lazy slob and sit on the couch all day watching sports.

You forget her birthday.

You remember her birthday, but you buy her a lame-ass present. On an old episode of *The Simpsons*, Homer bought Marge a bowling ball with *his* name on it. That's lame.

You don't talk to her. She interprets that as you not caring. If she thinks you don't care about her, she will start wondering why she's with you.

You don't listen to her. This is just as important as talking to her. A modern man has to know how to be a good listener if he wants to keep his woman happy. (Listening to her while watching a football game out of the corner of your eye is *not* listening to her.)

You refuse to do any housework. This is especially true if you're the one making most of the messes.

You don't give her any space to have time with her girlfriends. You talk to her with disdain and/or frustration in your voice.

Making sure you don't take your partner for granted is not difficult, but it does require your time and attention. Keep the love alive by being attentive to your lover's needs. No one needs lavish gifts bestowed on them daily or weekly. But small gestures of affection can do wonders in keeping the love alive.

Love Magnet Rule #101

Treat your lover as you wish to be treated.

This is the Golden Rule. There is no better way to honor the man or woman you love than to treat them exactly as you want to be treated.

You want to be loved and respected? Then love and respect your partner. You want your lover to treat you with kindness? Then treat him or her with kindness.

It's as simple as that. The Golden Rule, "Do unto others as you would have them do unto you," is the single best piece of human relationship advice ever given. It works if you're looking for love, in a loving relationship, or attempting to behave like an enlightened human being.

Treat your partner exactly as you want to be treated, and you might just live happily ever after with the love of your dreams.

THE END

Thank You

Thank you for reading my book. If you enjoyed it, please take a moment to leave me a review.

Chad Stone

For more information about Chad Stone, including his other books, visit www.chadstone.us.

Acknowledgments

I would like to thank everyone who helped in the writing of this book.

First, thanks to my wife, Krista, for her love, support, patience, kindness, and everything else she freely and generously gives to me every day. Without her, this book would not have been possible.

Many thanks to the family members and friends who make life so wonderful in every way.

Thanks to all of the men and women who shared their dating and relationship experiences with me. All of you (and there are many of you) helped to fill this book with valuable insights.

I would like to thank Ken Wilson for another great book cover design. Not only is he a good friend, but he does great work. Thanks also to Joni Wilson (no relation to Ken) for doing a great job of editing the manuscript and helping me look good.

And thanks to everyone who bought and read this book. Writing a book is a labor of love, and what makes it especially rewarding is the feedback from all of you who enjoy it.

Thank you all.

About the Author

Chad Stone is a dating and relationships success story. After his first marriage ended in divorce, he bravely entered the world of single adulthood and vowed to learn everything he could about dating, relationships, and finding love.

Mr. Stone interviewed singles of both genders to get insights about what women and men want in a love partner. He discovered that women and men want many of the same things, but women and men go about finding love in very different ways. So Chad interviewed dozens of men and women to find out what works and what doesn't work when searching for a romantic partner. He researched online dating to learn how to write an online profile that's guaranteed to get attention—and how to go from a "wink" to a date. As part of his research, he attended dating events including "speed dating" evenings and dating mixers. He became an expert in love.

Mr. Stone's research resulted in *The Love Magnet Rules: 101 Tips for Meeting, Dating, and Keeping a New Love*. In addition to this book, Chad Stone also shares dating and relationship advice on his blog at www.ChadStone.us. He is a frequent dating and relationships contributor to Boomeon.com and other sites. Chad Stone lives with his wife in Santa Fe, New Mexico.

Connect with Me

www.ChadStone.us

chad@chadstone.us

www.facebook.com/ChadStoneAuthor

@chadstone99

www.soulmatemedia.com

Made in the USA
Charleston, SC
21 July 2015